Japanese society

Lewis Henry Morgan Lecture Series

Japanese society

Tradition, self, and the social order

Robert J. Smith
Cornell University

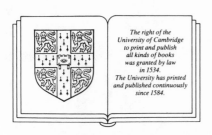

The right of the
University of Cambridge
to print and publish
all kinds of books
was granted by law
in 1534.
The University has printed
and published continuously
since 1584.

Cambridge University Press
Cambridge
London   New York   New Rochelle
Melbourne   Sydney

Published by the Press Syndicate of the University of Cambridge
The Pitt Building, Trumpington Street, Cambridge CB2 1RP
32 East 57th Street, New York, NY 10022, USA
10 Stamford Road, Oakleigh, Melbourne 3166, Australia

© Cambridge University Press 1983

First published 1983
First paperback edition 1985

Printed in the United States of America

Library of Congress Cataloging in Publication Data
Smith, Robert John, 1927–

Japanese society.

(Lewis Henry Morgan lectures series)
Bibliography: p.
Includes index.
1. Japan–Social conditions.   2. Social structure–
Japan.   I. Title.   II. Series.
HN723 S59 983 306'0952 83-7498
ISBN 0 521 25843 X hard covers
ISBN 0 521 31552 2 paperback

To my mother, Fern J. Smith,
and to the memory of my father, Will D. Smith,
in partial repayment of an unrepayable debt

Contents

Foreword

When the Lewis Henry Morgan Lectures began in 1963, none of those involved foresaw the variety of intellectual fare they would provide from year to year. (The connection of Lewis Henry Morgan with the University of Rochester and the initiation of the Morgan Lectures in 1963 are briefly discussed in the Foreword to Professor Meyer Fortes's *Kinship and the Social Order* [Aldine, 1969]). Robert Smith's lectures, presented here, are another striking example of the kinds of analysis and synthesis successive lectures have offered appreciative audiences.

Before World War II, anthropological materials on Japan in English were practically nonexistent, with Embree's *Suye Mura* a lonely precursor of the flood of research published in the postwar years. Anthropology has been accompanied by Western scholars in other disciplines, and the readily available literature on Japan in English alone is now beyond the compass of all, save an accomplished few. The variety of approaches and differing interpretations call for guidance, and this volume provides that and more.

Professor Smith's lectures constitute one of those remarkable – and rare – contributions that does not just present an array of data and conclusions (in this instance drawn from many years of research in and on Japan and Japanese society and culture). He goes beyond this, offering general principles of critical importance, to be seen in operation not only in Japan's past but in the modern state as well. He invites novices to explore further, and will undoubtedly provoke experts of diverse persuasions to debate with him or to rethink their own conclusions.

Those who were privileged to hear Professor Smith's lectures (on March 18, 20, 25, and 27, 1980) delivered with rare urbanity and clarity will now be able to hear him again as they read. His wider audience may hear echoes of the spoken word. And all his readers will be able to pause, reflect, and pursue the many and varied avenues of thought he suggests.

ALFRED HARRIS
Editor
The Lewis Henry Morgan Lectures

Acknowledgments

The lectures on which this book is based were delivered at the University of Rochester in March 1980. Alfred Harris, who graciously introduced me to the audience that proved to be remarkably faithful in staying with me throughout the series, was the perfect host. To Grace G. Harris, chair of the Department of Anthropology, and to the members of the department who made my wife and me feel welcome for the duration of our stay, we extend our thanks.

Several people were kind enough to read the manuscript of the lectures as they were originally delivered. Harumi Befu, Bernard Bernier, James A. Boon, Walter D. Edwards, Davydd J. Greenwood, Michael Kammen, and Stephen P. Nussbaum offered valuable and perhaps oversupportive advice. William B. Hauser made extensive and incisive comments that have helped shape several passages in the final version of the manuscript. I am grateful to them all, and wish to absolve them of any blame for the shortcomings that survived their best efforts to dissuade me of a line of argument or emphasis in interpretation.

I undertook the task of revision of the manuscript while a visiting professor at the National Museum of Ethnology in Osaka, Japan, and am greatly indebted to Director General Umesao Tadao and Professor Sofue Takao, director of the

First Research Department, for extending to me the use of the remarkably advanced facilities of that institution during the fall of 1982.

ROBERT J. SMITH

A note to the reader: Japanese names in the text are given with the surname first (Maruyama Masao) except where the individual is a longtime resident of the United States (Masao Miyoshi) or American-born (Harumi Befu). The bibliography, which is rather long for so short a book, is intended to provide guidance for those who wish to pursue topics and issues raised in the text.

Introduction

In 1871, Lewis Henry Morgan published his monumental study *Systems of Consanguinity and Affinity of the Human Family,* in which he attacked a problem that still commands the attention of a segment of the anthropological profession. He was concerned with devising a system by means of which kinship terminologies could be classified. Amassing information from many sources and collecting some himself, he assembled what he believed to be overwhelming evidence for the existence of two major types of terminology. The classificatory system, characteristic of primitive societies, merges lineal and collateral kin terminologically. The descriptive system, that of civilized societies, distinguishes between lineal and collateral kin by use of different terms.

It is not my purpose to reenter the continuing debate as to the accuracy or utility of Morgan's formulation.[1] I will, rather, take note of the extraordinary fact that one of the sets of kin terms recorded in the monograph is the Japanese. On the basis of the material presented there, Morgan characterizes the Japanese as evolutionarily primitive by virtue of their having a classificatory system of kinship terminology. They do not, nor is there any evidence that they ever did, possess such a system of kin terms,[2] but I am less interested in the reasons for Morgan's error than in the circumstances that led to the inclusion

1

of the Japanese case at all, for it was Morgan himself who collected the information in Rochester, New York, in May 1867. Reflect for a moment how unlikely an event this is. Only fourteen years earlier Commodore Perry's squadron had entered Japanese waters, breaching irrevocably the barrier of isolation that had sealed off the country for more than two hundred years. Japan, quite well known throughout Europe in the sixteenth and seventeenth centuries, had become so indistinct to Western eyes that Perry apparently was not even aware that the military shogun with whom he indirectly negotiated was not the emperor of Japan, yet the distinction between the two offices had once been common knowledge in the West.

In 1867, then, a year before the Meiji Restoration, Morgan reports that he had brought to him a Japanese "troupe of adventurers" who were performing (what, he does not say) in American cities. They must have been among the first Japanese to pass through upstate New York, and it is an indication of the degree to which Morgan was seized by the imperative that drives all ethnographers that he felt compelled to add the Japanese to his roster of societies. It was from their interpreter, one Kawabe Mankichi, that he elicited the set of terms that graces the tables of his monograph.

A search of the local newspapers for early May 1867 (Morgan's own notes bear the dates of May 13 and 14) reveals not only the identity of the troupe, but also that their performances excited considerable interest and expressions of unbounded admiration for their skill. Both the *Rochester Daily Democrat* and the *Rochester Daily Union and Advertiser* carried the somewhat overwrought announcement shown on page 3. The *Union and Advertiser* reviewed the first performance in its May 7 edition, and the *Democrat* printed no fewer than four stories about the group between May 8 and 11. Unhappily, the name of Morgan's informant appears in none of them.

Corinthian Hall
Rochester, N.Y.
The Best for Lecturers, Concerts, Operas, etc.
Samu'l Wilder, Proprietor
Howard T. Fleming, Agent
50 Arcade
Corinthian Hall
Maguire's Imperial
Japanese Troupe
Six Nights and Matinees Only
Commencing Monday Eve'ng, May 6, 1867

This Troupe consists of the most UNIQUE, and WONDERFUL JUGGLERS, BALANCERS, MAGICIANS, ACROBATS, and MUSICIANS from Jeddo, Japan, being the first private citizens ever permitted to leave the Empire.

The same Troupe which has created so much excitement in Boston, Springfield, Hartford, Philadelphia, and Washington. This being an entirely Japanese entertainment, the stage will be conducted in precisely the same manner as in Japan.

Admission 50 cts.   Reserved seats 75 cts.

In the course of the interview, however, Morgan was careful to inquire into Kawabe's background. Like any other ethnographer working in similar circumstances of isolation, he could not have known that his informant was lying to him. Kawabe represented himself as a member of a warrior family of high rank (*hatamoto*), an origin so implausible for a member of a traveling troupe of jugglers and acrobats that the claim can be dismissed out of hand. I am not simply guessing, for on internal evidence alone, the data recorded by Morgan can be seen to be the product of a combination of faulty interviewing on the part of the ethnographer and the responses of an informant of humble social origins with little formal education.[3]

There is, of course, no way Morgan could have known or

discovered the truth about Kawabe's background, but even had he done so, there was as yet no place in the study of kinship for the realization that social class, educational attainment, and interactive context may crucially affect the terminologies for kin that members of a given society employ. I will return from time to time to this and related issues in discussing several facets of Japanese society, but let me conclude this preamble by noting the peculiarly fitting identity of the man who brought Kawabe Mankichi to Lewis Henry Morgan. He is identified only as the entrepreneur who had organized the troupe's American tour — a Mr. Smith.

Because few of my readers share my longstanding concern with Japanese society and are not therefore regularly exposed to the outpouring of literature on the subject, an explanation of the tone I have taken in the following pages is in order. There are many views of Japan and many bitter disputes about the true character of that society, which is, after all, a very complex one. Some argue that the whole recent history of the country is one long tale of unrelieved betrayal of its people by successive repressive regimes. Others find in its achievements sufficient grounds for endorsement of the techniques employed in realizing them. Still others take the position that when all is said and done, there is more in the record to extol than to condemn. The disagreements are fundamental, obviously, but we do not find foreign observers aligned on one side of the debate against Japanese scholars and commentators on the other. Nevertheless, there is an unmistakable tendency for the Japanese to be far more critical of their society on the whole than are the foreigners who study it.

Among our Japanese colleagues are many who lament the failure of their compatriots to achieve social or psychological maturity, an outcome that can be obtained, they seem to feel, only when Japanese society is at last rid of that very tradition that is one of the themes of this book. In this regard, the attitude of the Japanese intellectual is one of black despair. Yet to many of us who come from other societies, Japan today seems a remarkably civil place, and its people more cheerfully optimistic for the future than are the citizens of most other nations, who probably have more objective cause to be so.

On every hand there is disagreement over the interpretation of behavior. What seems to some to be politeness is read as obsequiousness by others; what in one view is a passion for order is in another held to be hapless conformity; the dedication to work that so excites the admiration of many is elsewhere construed as mindless surrender to paternalistic exploitation; even the most modest degree of self-assertion that is lauded by those who hope for change is denounced as rampant egoism by those whose goal is stability; what one finds to be expression of individuality, another takes to be evidence of unbridled selfishness. Those who comment favorably on the achievements of Japanese society are accused of failing to pay sufficient attention to the high price paid for them; observers who stress their formidable personal and social costs are derided for their blindness to the positive social gains that have been made.

Nowhere, however, is the disagreement more basic than that over the answer to the obvious question: How different is this, the only major industrial society yet to emerge from outside the Western tradition? Those who think it not different at all are positively offended by suggestions that it is so in any significant degree.[4] Those who hold the opposite view argue, as I do, that in fact it is a different kind of society. The difference lies less in its organizations and institutions than in the way all of its history shows how the Japanese think about man and society and the relationship between the two.

It would be remarkable indeed if at the end of only one short century the Japanese, alone among the peoples of the world, had managed to divest themselves of the legacy of their past[5] — which, we cannot be reminded too often, is not based in any of its particulars on the philosophical or religious heritage of the Western tradition. Of course Japan is unlike its Western counterparts. How could it be otherwise? Had Japan no high-speed trains, no great industrial cities whose streets are choked with domestically produced automobiles, and no preeminence in many fields of technology, the point would hardly need to be made. But because Japan has all of these and more, it seems to many that in the process of their acquisition, it must have developed into a particular kind of society. Which is to say it must be like other societies with which it shares so many technological and economic characteristics. I find that view less than compelling, for it is reminiscent of a time when grand social theories were in rather more abundant supply than they have been in recent years, and in better repute.

None of this means that Japan cannot be understood. It means only that in order to understand it, we must wrench ourselves out of well-worn ruts of assumption and expectation. I shall take the admittedly dangerous course of presenting a normative picture of a complex industrial society that I believe to be based on premises fundamentally different from our own. The result of this exercise, I hope, will be to provide evidence in support of the claim that there are alternative ways in which a mass society can be constructed. This is hardly as extraordinary an assertion as it may seem at first blush. Does anyone today really believe that all the industrial societies of the Western tradition itself are identical? Surely not. We know that the French and British bureaucracies are unlike one another in many respects and that both differ from the American. It is clear that Italy and Sweden and Australia are not stamped in the same mold. Why, then, should it so offend to suggest that Japan is different from them all?

In the course of a conference I recently attended, the discussion of development turned inevitably to this very question. One of those present cited approvingly the results of a long list of studies that seemed to him to show that the decision-making process in Japan, contrary to the usual claim that it is unfamiliar in many of its particulars, is in fact quite like that used in the West. A second participant, delighted with this confirmation of his own cherished convictions, exclaimed with evident satisfaction: "There, you see? The longer we study the Japanese, the more human they become!" What he was really saying, I submit, is that by diligent effort the Japanese can be made to seem more and more like us. It is one of the purposes of this book to show why we are driven to seek that reassurance.

.

1

The Creation of Tradition

"We have no history. Our history begins today."
A Japanese to the German physician Erwin Baelz, 1876.[1]

The record of the past exists to be exploited, rephrased, abridged, or ignored. What is not in the record can be invented. Examples of all of these processes abound in the modern world, as the reader of any daily newspaper will know. The Japanese, I think, are not particularly unusual in the way they manipulate the record of their past, but it will be my contention that they are unusually adept at it. I also believe that a flexible approach to history may well prove to be a great advantage to any society faced with the necessity of making very rapid institutional transformations. As a Japanese proverb has it, the winds may fell the massive oak, but bamboo, bent even to the ground, will spring upright after the passage of the storm. Such resilience in social systems may be rare, I suspect, and even those that possess it run the risk of destruction if the appeals for change are grounded in a complete falsification of the past and violate the basic principles on which the system rests. In this regard, the Japanese uses of their past for present purposes commend themselves to our attention.

The geographic location of Japan has much to do with the peculiarities of its cultural history, for it lies far off the continent of Asia, more isolated from it than the British Isles from

9

Europe. It is a kind of cul de sac, the terminus of the successive waves of influence that have washed into it over the millennia. Japanese culture today embraces traditions developed elsewhere in highly diverse times and places—the Buddhism of India out of China and Korea, Confucianism, and the institutions, arts, and philosophies of China and much of the Western world. Yet, as the physicist Yukawa has noted, their assimilation has been so complete that contemporary Japanese culture oddly lacks the cosmopolitan flavor that the diversity of its sources would seem to dictate for it (1973:15–16). Assimilation is probably not the proper term. Perhaps incorporation is better, for Japan is in some ways like a tidal pool, isolated for long periods from the source of all it contains, a place where accommodation, transformation, and amalgamation proceed uninterrupted until the next tidal sweep irrevocably alters its composition.

There are dangers in any analogy, of course, but let me demonstrate the utility of this one by reference to the Imperial Rescript on Education, promulgated in 1890, less than a generation after the fall of the Tokugawa shogunate and the Meiji Restoration of 1868:

Know ye, Our Subjects:
Our Imperial Ancestors have founded our Empire on a basis broad and everlasting and have deeply and firmly implanted virtue; Our subjects ever united in loyalty and filial piety have from generation to generation illustrated the beauty thereof. This is the glory of the fundamental character of Our Empire, and herein also lies the source of Our education. Ye, Our subjects, be filial to your parents, affectionate to your brothers and sisters; as husbands and wives be harmonious, as friends true; bear yourselves in modesty and moderation; extend your benevolence to all; pursue learning and cultivate arts, and thereby develop intellectual faculties and perfect moral powers; furthermore advance public good and promote common interest; always respect the Constitution and observe the laws; should emergency arise, offer yourselves courageously to the State;

and thus guard and maintain the prosperity of Our Imperial Throne coeval with heaven and earth. So shall ye not only be Our good and faithful subjects, but render illustrious the best traditions of your forefathers.

The Way here set forth is indeed the teaching bequeathed by Our Imperial Ancestors, to be observed alike by Their Descendants and the subjects, infallible for all ages and true in all places. It is Our wish to lay it to heart in all reverence, in common with you, Our subjects, that we may thus attain to the same virtue. (Tsunoda et al. 1958: 646–7)

This document, representing the final victory of the conservative elements in the new Japanese government, early assumed an almost talismanic character. For the fifty-five years following its promulgation to the end of the Greater East Asia War, it was read aloud in full by the school principal at periodic ceremonies, was made the subject of countless exegeses, and its sentiments worked into the textbooks of ethics and morals used in the primary and middle schools. At the heart of both official and popular commentaries on the rescript, we encounter a point of view that enjoyed a great vogue at the time. It is derived from an entirely unexpected source, the writings of the all but forgotten English metaphysical philosopher T. H. Green.[2] Many of the leading educators of the time were strongly influenced by his writings and sought to introduce them into the curriculum in a variety of ways. The eminent educator Yoshida Seichi wrote that Green's doctrine of "self-regulation" recommended itself particularly for adoption by the Japanese, and from it culled two central propositions: "Man's worth is judged by the degree of his effort to approximate his existing self to an ideal self." He further maintained that the ideal "appears in the consciousness of each man as the social, and the ideal for one's self consists in the ideal for society" (Hirai 1979:118). It is difficult to imagine a theory of the relationship between the individual subject and the state more congenial to the aims of conservatives whose design it was to gain ever tighter control of the apparatus of the state.

For the foreign reader, however, the full import of the rescript will be missed without a careful examination of the
origins of its principal themes and the uses to which it was
ultimately put. Let us stand back from the document for a
moment, therefore, and take a long look at the institution of
the imperial house. For of all the features of Japanese society
that exemplify the adeptness at the use of the past for present
purposes, that which has proved most durable because most
infinitely flexible is surely the imperial institution.

Consider for a moment its putative history. Whether or
not the legendary and semilegendary emperors are included in
the reckoning, it is easily the world's longest royal dynasty. The
present emperor is the 124th of his line, which traces its descent
from Amaterasu, the sun goddess. The historical record suggests, however, that there have been two breaks in the succession, first in the second century and again in the early sixth,
when the twenty-sixth emperor Keitai seized the throne,[3] and
even he married a princess from the royal line he had displaced.
The rewriters of history have generally concealed these dynastic
breaks by genealogical manipulation, but even if they are
granted, it is nonetheless true that all subsequent occupants of
the throne are indisputably the patrilineal descendants of Keitai. Alone among Japanese families, the imperial family bears
no surname and to it alone is forbidden the otherwise common
practice of adoption. In other ways, however, it is not particularly remarkable, not even in its claim to divine descent, for
most of the great political and military houses of Japanese history, and not a few lesser ones, have identified as their ancestor
of origin one or another of the deities named in the myths of
the Age of the Gods.

Given the nature of the claim to the throne, usurpation is
simply not possible, for it is occupied not by divine right or the
Mandate of Heaven, but by virtue of authentic genealogical
descent from the divine founder of the line. Indeed, the Japa-

nese imperial house advances the rather unusual and possibly unique claim of being able to trace its ancestry back in cosmic time before the establishment of the state over which it was to exercise sovereignty. Yet these divine kings were divested of political, secular power for a full seven hundred years between the inception of warrior rule with the founding of the Kamakura shogunate in 1185 and the Meiji Restoration of 1868. Why, then, did the institution persist, and why does it still exist? The answer lies, I think, in its very long and complete uncoupling from the exercise of secular, political power and its role as the ultimate source of legitimacy for those who sought to wield that power in its name.[4]

It is noteworthy that in the early years of Japan's modern century, following the Meiji Restoration, translations of official documents used the transliteration *tennō* to refer to the head of state. The instinct behind this decision was right, but later when the government opted for translation instead, the unfortunate choice was "emperor" rather than "king." As a consequence, the nature of the position has long been obscured. For to the foreign reader, the word "emperor" conjures up images of pomp and the public display of immense wealth and power, both quite antithetical to the role and functions of the *tennō* throughout most of Japanese history. Let us look for a moment at those functions in the period prior to the Restoration.

The Tokugawa shoguns, third and last of the military houses to rule the country, argued early in their period of dominance that although they were the legitimate rulers, the emperor remained above them but did not govern. Later they claimed legitimacy as his proxies or deputies. Ieyasu, who founded the Tokugawa shogunate at the end of a century of civil wars, had in the early seventeenth century seized upon neo–Confucianism as the ethical system most likely effectively to serve his aim to unify the country under his leadership. Particularly congenial was Chu Hsi's teaching on the

Way of the King, who ruled by the Mandate of Heaven, for Japanese Confucianists equated the king with the shogun, the secular ruler. In this formulation, however, there was no place at all for the theory of the divine authority of the emperor, posing a problem that was to preoccupy philosophers of the Tokugawa era for 250 years. Their resolutions of the apparent contradiction differed in detail and even in major thrust, but it is safe to say that by and large they resorted to the Confucian idiom in their justification of the shogun's position and to native Japanese tradition — most conveniently called Shinto (The Way of the Gods)—for explication of that of the emperor.[5]

This solution — if solution it be — is of a kind frequently encountered in Japan. There appears to be a marked tendency to receive ideas and concepts from diverse sources,[6] and to incorporate them into the existing system without much concern for their compatibility: "Ideas are for the Japanese nothing more than tools that can be used for various purposes. If a saw does not do the job, you can use an axe. In the same way, if Confucianism does not give the desired result, resort may be had to Buddhism" (Y. Noda 1976:170), or we might add, to Shinto. Nevertheless, by the mid-nineteenth century, recognition of the obvious incompatibility of the two legitimating systems, one of shogunal rule and the other of imperial reign, provided the impetus for the formulation of a theory of government that was in the end to bring down the shogunate.

The group of scholars in the Mito domain, whose influence on the course of action that was later pursued cannot be overestimated, concluded that the shoguns had in fact usurped imperial power and therefore must go. It is a fine irony that the last shogun, Yoshinobu, was to claim that he acted in accordance with the teachings handed down to him by the founder of his line, Tokugawa Ieyasu. He was, he maintained, following the doctrine of the Supreme Duty of Loyalty and

Filial Piety in ending Tokugawa rule. There is a double irony here, for the final synthesis that had left no place for the shogun had been arrived at by the scholars of the domain of Yoshinobu's own father, Tokugawa Nariaki, lord of Mito. The leaders of the movement to oust the Tokugawa took as one of their many slogans *ōsei fukko* (the restoration of the emperor), but it is important for our purposes to note that *fukko* means literally "to restore antiquity." The emperor had not ruled for centuries, but had remained the symbolic embodiment of national independence, historic continuity, unity, and harmony within the government and between rulers and ruled (Webb 1965:187). Thus, he was immensely important to the leaders of the Restoration movement, for he alone could give them the legitimacy they so desperately required, as his predecessors had done to the three shogunal houses for the preceding seven centuries. They therefore treated him with great ceremonial respect, and by so doing were able to assert continuity in the name of the sovereign while in fact they pursued a course for which there were no true precedents (Beasley 1972:302).

It is in the Imperial Rescript on Education that continuity was asserted with a vengeance, marshaling the Shinto and Confucian traditions into what is simultaneously an assertion of unassailable legitimacy, a definition of the virtues of the subject, and a claim for the unique character of the Japanese state. The authority for the assertion of unassailable legitimacy derives from "the teaching bequeathed to us by Our Imperial Ancestors," a reference to the vow (*shinchoku*) made by the sun goddess when she despatched her grandson, Ninigi-no-mikoto, to earth. She promised him that the line of his descendants would flourish, and it was his great-grandson Jimmu who became the first emperor of Japan (Earl 1964:47n). Only a year before the rescript was issued, the Meiji emperor had granted a constitution to the Japanese people. The preamble makes the same claim, beginning: "Having, by virtue of the glories of Our Ancestors, ascended the Throne of a lineal succession unbroken for ages eternal . . ." and further asserts that "The right of sovereignty of the State, We have inherited from Our Ancestors, and We shall bequeath it to Our descendants."[7]

The rescript thus echoes the constitution, but it does much more. Drawing on the synthesis of Western positivism and Confucian humanism produced in the 1880s by Nishimura Shigeki (1828–1902), the drafters of the rescript defined the virtues of the subject in terms provided by Confucianism's central truth as Nishimura saw it: "It taught that the meaning of social life lay not in seeking salvation in another world . . . but in cultivating relationships among members of society built on trust, a fundamental sense of one's humaneness, and, above all, a commitment to loyal action on behalf of others" (Najita 1980:98–9). What came to be known as the Way of the Subject is thus defined exclusively in terms of the Confucian virtues of loyalty and filial piety, but phrased quite as though they were equally an aspect of the ancient Japanese tradition. For Buddhism there was no place at all. As we will see, it was only twenty years later that the ultimate fusion was made in the ethics and morals textbooks of the public school system, where from 1910 to 1945 it was held that imperial loyalty and filial piety were one and the same. The household and the state had been effectively encapsulated into an indivisible sacred entity of sentiment and ceremony.

Finally, the reference in the rescript to "the fundamental character of Our Empire" is a translation of the word *kokutai*.[8] Found in ancient Chinese writings, but given currency in Japan not much before the early nineteenth century, it means something like the unique characteristics of Japan, "an inner essence or mystical force residing in the Japanese nation as a result of the Sun Goddess's vow" (Earl 1964:236).[9]

I have dwelt on these matters at such length because they relate directly to the uses of the past. I have already suggested that the manipulation of the past, for whatever purposes, will succeed largely to the extent that care is taken that the appeals for change reinforce or at least do not violate the basic principles and sentiments on which the system rests. Could the founders of the modern Japanese state have created these appeals out of whole cloth and still have led the people where they wanted them to go? I think not. It is important to see that the rhetoric of the Meiji oligarchs is at once revolutionary in its intent and profoundly conservative in its idiom. Seeking nationalist revolution, they called it imperial restoration. Had they merely falsified the past, rather than adroitly combining and reordering some of its salient themes, they surely would have failed in their efforts to persuade the Japanese people of the legitimacy of their position and their goals. What they could not do was jettison it.

The key to legitimation was the imperial institution, and the leaders and ideologues of the Meiji Restoration were concerned to formulate a plausible definition of the role of the emperor in the government and his relationship to society. On October 23, 1868, in what is commonly called a Shinto court ceremony, the young emperor selected a slip of paper from among a number placed before him. It bore the two characters "bright" and "rule," and thus gave his reign its name — Meiji. It is testimony to the highly incorporative nature of the system that the characters were taken from a quotation in the *Book of Changes* (Jansen 1970:95), the ancient diviner's manual claimed by the later Chinese Confucianists as one of the Five Classics. It had come to Japan centuries earlier, and was so thoroughly bound up with Japanese conceptions of the cosmic order that it had long played a critical role in the essentially Shinto idiom of the court ritual designed to select a reign name of auspiciousness and felicity.

This moment in Japanese history thus offers insight into a long-established tradition of incorporation, but there remains the question of the relationship of the emperor to his subjects, over whom he was to rule. It has seemed to many interpreters of the true import of the Meiji Restoration essential to show all the ways in which the imperial institution was forced on a hapless people by the manipulative wielders of power.[10] Although it is true that the new government was at some pains throughout the early part of the Meiji period to establish some unprecedented associations and sentiments with which to bind the people to the emperor, we are fortunate to have an eyewitness account of a crucial event in the history of the Restoration that speaks to a fundamental continuity. In November 1868 the emperor set out from the old imperial capital at Kyoto to visit his new one, recently renamed Tokyo. Some months later he was to take up residence there in the former palace of the shoguns, in a gesture designed to symbolize the fusion of secular and sacred power. On his first visit, he entered his new capital in a palanquin of a sort probably not seen outside the confines of the imperial palace for nearly a millennium. An account of the event, which occurred on November 26, was carried in the *Japan Times*: "The following extract will be read with interest as descriptive of a part of the last purely Japanese pageant either Japan or the world is like to see:"[11]

After about half of these [the daimios and *kuges*] had passed, with their attendants, led horses, guards and baggage, with occasional bodies of troops, came the Prince of Bizen, in charge of two square boxes borne high upon men's shoulders, and covered with a red and yellow damask silk. These were believed to contain the insignia or regalia, and small shrines for their safe custody had been erected at all the halting-places along the road. After these rode Uwajima, the Minister for Foreign Affairs, and then we saw approaching the Hō-ō-ren or phoenix car.

This is a black lacquered palanquin, about six feet square, and with a dome-shaped roof; the front is closed only by curtains, and in the centre of each side is a latticed window, through which it was possible to see that it held no one. The Mikado is supposed to travel in it, but has really a more comfortable palanquin. On the summit is a splendid image, apparently of gold, of the Hō-ō, or phoenix, a fabulous bird, with the head and body of a peacock and the spreading plume-like tail of the magnificent copper pheasant of Japan turned up over its head. From the four corners depend red silk ropes two inches thick, held each by three men. These and the bearers of the car, which is carried high upon their shoulders and on a frame which raises its base some six feet from the ground, were on Thursday all dressed in bright yellow silk, and wore a curious circular ornament of feathers at each ear eight inches in diameter, like two outspread fan frames placed together. There were fully sixty of them immediately surrounding the Hō-ō-ren, and the effect of the group, with the brilliant sun lighting up the sheen of the silk and the glitter of the lacquer, was very gorgeous and indescribably strange, comparable to nothing ever seen in any other part of the world. And now a great silence fell upon the people. Far as the eye could see on either side, the roadsides were densely packed with the crouching populace, in their ordinary position when any official of rank passes by.... As the phoenix car ... with its halo of glittering attendants came on ... the people without order or signal turned their faces to the earth, ... no man moved or spoke for a space, and all seemed to hold their breath for very awe, as the mysterious presence, on whom few are privileged to look and live, was passing by.

Another observer wrote of that same occasion, "The silence that prevailed among the assembled multitudes, during his passage, was really something that might be felt. . . . [I]t was impressive in the extreme. All the people bowed down as he approached, but this was the last time I ever saw them do so for any great man. The next time I witnessed a procession in which the Mikado figured, all was changed . . . ; His Majesty dressed in European costume rode in a carriage, free to be gazed on by all beholders; and the people had been notified that the . . . bowing-down would not be enforced" (Black

1883:II,236). Taken together, these accounts provide us with two valuable insights into the nature of the imperial institution at the outset of Japan's modern period. It will surely have struck the reader as astonishing that the palanquin that entered Tokyo in 1868 was, in fact, quite empty. It should also be noted that the procession has much in common with the great trains of the feudal lords (*daimyō*) of the Tokugawa period that moved along the postroads of Japan in accordance with the requirements of the policy of alternate residence in the shogun's capital.[12] Accustomed to making obeisance to these figures of power for more than two hundred years, the people perhaps only complied with long-established traditional usage. What was different, however, was the inclusion in this procession of the symbolic presence of the emperor, and we may be sure that no multitude would have turned out to watch yet another daimyo train pass by. That the emperor and the regalia were concealed from view is quite beside the point; the passage of the symbols of the imperial institution, rather than his person, signaled that the world would never be the same.

The second insight is to be found in the comment, written only fifteen years later, that this awesome procession marked the end of something. For when the emperor emerged from his palace in the new capital, he had been transformed into a monarch of another kind, dressed in the foreign style and riding in an open carriage for all his subjects to see. This transformation is all the more remarkable if we consider for a moment the immediate history of the imperial house in the Tokugawa period.

Between 1586 and 1866, there were fifteen occupants of the throne, two of them women. What the unfortunate use of the English word "emperor" obscures is that they were divine kings in the classic sense, and the essential role they alone could play was the equally classic one of conducting the rites and ceremonies that both define and reaffirm the cosmic order. Their persons so sacred that they were not permitted to touch the earth, they remained hidden from the eyes of their subjects, who made pilgrimages to the shrine of the imperial ancestors at Ise, but did not worship the persons of the emperors themselves. Indeed, their seclusion was so complete that between 1626 and 1863 none left the precincts of the palace except when fires and other emergencies required that the palace itself be relocated (Webb 1965:172–3). When the young Meiji emperor visited Osaka in April 1868, he became the first Japanese monarch in almost three hundred years to see the ocean.

It is a tribute to the oligarchs that so identified was the emperor with the state a half-century later, that when Crown Prince Hirohito (the present emperor) was permitted to go abroad in 1921, it was the cause of considerable misgiving at many levels of Japanese society. It was another half-century later, in 1971, that he became the first emperor ever to leave the islands, an event that is less a tribute to the rise of a cosmopolitan internationalism than an acknowledgment of his highly attenuated relationship to the state. It is one of the lesser ironies of history that on this occasion the Japanese government was rocked by the gaffe of President Nixon, who greeted him at Anchorage as "the first reigning monarch of Japan" to set foot on American soil. The slip was particularly embarrassing because it was the United States that had pressed on the Japanese a constitution that recognizes the emperor as symbol of the state, who does not reign. Today, stripped of both power and sovereignty, "the emperor serves only in the most disembodied of the manifestations with which he was historically endowed, as symbol of his country's moral consciousness" (J. W. Hall 1968:64).

A century earlier, however, the imperial institution had been a symbol of enormous potential power. It is small wonder that the leaders of the new government relied so heavily on the presumed divine authority of the occupant of the throne, and on the assertion that their policies derived from ancient native practice and teachings. Throughout the debate over the constitution and the structure of the new government, while Western theory and example were assiduously studied, and competing positions buttressed by appeals to Anglo-French or German concepts, the debate was in reality "essentially concerned with traditional predispositions" to such an extent that ultimately every spokesman felt moved to legitimate his program by reference to traditional sources. So great was the concern to clothe new concepts in traditional garb that the notion of popular sovereignty, drawn largely from the writings of Rousseau and the study of English practice, came represented as derived from the teaching of Mencius (Jansen 1970:111).

Even the formation of the modern cabinet system was rationalized in just such a manner. On December 22, 1885, all the traditional court offices were abolished and it was announced that there would henceforth be a prime minister and several ministers of state. The retiring *dajōdaijin* (chancellor, chief minister) held that the establishment of a cabinet marked a reversion to the ancient Japanese political theory that the emperor ruled personally, with his ministers serving as his advisers and consultants (Beckmann 1957:75). Never mind that both the cabinet and the character of the relationship of the ministers to the emperor were closely modeled on the Prussian, as the oligarchs and their political enemies both knew well enough. I am here concerned with the uses of the past, of which there could be no clearer example.

In this connection it is pertinent to consider the role of one Hermann Roesler, without doubt the most influential foreign political adviser to the Meiji government.[13] A distinguished German economist and jurist, Roesler was hired in

1878 as adviser to the Japanese Foreign Office, and soon extended his influence to all ministries involved in the creation of the new legal and administrative systems that the times demanded. Deeply suspicious of the growing movement for popular rights, he allied himself solidly with the conservative figures in the government. There is ample evidence to show that for these men, the motivation for political action was lodged securely in devotion to the emperor, a characteristic that particularly recommended them to their foreign adviser. Roesler, who admired their absolute conviction and applauded their aspirations, was easily convinced that the monarchy was the foundation of Japanese national life and the only institution on which the new political order could possibly be built.

It is chiefly for this reason that in the Meiji Constitution, which is largely his work and thus reflects a rather liberal interpretation of the German school of monarchical constitutional law, every effort is made to place the emperor at the center, synthesizing imperial authority and the rights of the people. Where Roesler could not follow his Japanese colleagues was in their theory of the identity of the state and imperial power, which required the assertion of divine descent. Perhaps the most important of these men was Inoue Kowashi (1844–95) who was concerned to demonstrate the essential continuity of the national essence—the *kokutai*—by resorting to a highly selective reading of Japanese mytho-history. Committed to the Prussian model and frustrated by Roesler's balking, they sought to lend weight to their argument by seeking out far more conservative German advisers from among those who had not, like Roesler, opposed the promulgation of the Bismarck Constitution in their own land. They provided a highly satisfactory Western formula, and the framers of the Meiji Constitution emerged with a theory of the state as living historical entity. Whereas Roesler had posited an emperor who both reigned and ruled, they enthroned instead a figure "completely outside the real political order as numen, as a pure symbol of the divine order" (Siemes 1968:27).

As the time approached to promulgate the new constitution, there was substantial disagreement over how the formalities should be handled. There was by no means universal approbation of the activities of the oligarchs during the first twenty years of the Meiji period, and they had striven mightily to complete the document that would be the cornerstone of the new state as they envisaged it as far out of public view as was possible. It is entirely consistent with their record of utilization of the throne that they chose the time, place, and manner of promulgation with considerable care. The ceremony was held in 1889, on February 11, which is *kigensetsu*, the mythical date of the founding of the Japanese state upon the accession of the first emperor, Jimmu. They chose as the locale the imperial palace, where in a brief declaration to the small assemblage of government officials, men of affairs, and diplomatic representatives, the emperor granted a constitution to his people (Beckmann 1957:82–3). It was a master stroke, and publicists were to make much of the point that in Japan alone of the constitutional monarchies, the people had not had to wrest a constitution from the sovereign. Rather, the emperor had graciously deigned to grant them one.

Yet the ceremony of promulgation had hardly been the occasion for a public outpouring of joy; the public had no part in the event at all. The document had been prepared in secret by a very small group of men, and it had been put into effect without public discussion. This extraordinary circumstance suggests that there was a marked tension between the traditionalists and the modernists, the goals of the one being anathema to the other. They had disagreed about almost every other reform of the period up to this point. Yet for all the bitterness that characterized the political maneuvering following the Restoration, the Tokugawa state had been dismantled,

—not without bloodshed, to be sure—but certainly without the wholesale chaos of full-fledged civil war, which many had feared might well break out. The success of the transition can be accounted for if, as Thomas C. Smith has argued, we see that in the absence of an aristocratic defense of the old regime, there has been no ideological cleavage of any radical kind. "All . . . were more or less reformist, more or less traditional, and more or less modern. . . ." With respect to the idea of progress, it was the view of all that the past "was a barrier in some respects; in others a positive aid. Modernization appeared to most Japanese who thought about it at all, not as a process in which a life-or-death confrontation of traditional and modern took place, but as a dynamic blending of the two" (1961:382). I shall try to show in succeeding chapters how I believe this point of view to hold still in contemporary Japan. Furthermore, with respect to the uses to which the imperial institution was put, it is well to point out that the emperor, during the long centuries of seclusion in Kyoto, had been neither a scourge nor a burden to his people (J. W. Hall 1968:41). But more important, perhaps, because he held the throne by virtue of genealogical succession rather than mere right of possession, he exemplified one of the most fundamental of all Japanese conceptions of the nature of the world—that there is no recognized separation of the moral order from the actual (1968:29).

Such an attitude cannot but profoundly affect the behavior of the members of a society who subscribe to it, and one of the ways in which many observers have seen it to work out in contemporary Japan is in a thoroughgoing pragmatism. It is by no means a new development, as the following example illustrates. From the early seventeenth century, the great outlying feudal domain of Satsuma began to issue regulations called *shūmon tefuda aratame jōmoku* (Regulations for the Investigation of Religious Sects and Identification Tags), which were updated from time to time. The edition of 1852 has been translated and edited (Haraguchi et al. 1975) for the light it throws on the status system and social organization of the domain. Satsuma is often taken as the epitome of conservatism and traditionalism even in the context of the highly conservative and traditional Tokugawa polity, yet the author of the introduction to this study pays tribute to the highly pragmatic character of the documents in question: "So long as the traditions served their purpose, they were maintained, but when . . . [domain] interests dictated a change, the rules and regulations were modified without apologies [in edicts] singularly devoid of moralistic or ideological rationalization."[14]

For present-day Japan, we are reminded that this kind of pragmatism is not the philosophers' essentially negative reaction to idealism, but rather "the positive expression of an instinctive vitalism, it implies actions which are taken when following the hidden and continuous flow of life's forces and rhythms" (Maraini 1975:70). And Nakamura Hajime (1964: 362) concludes his survey of the Japanese "way of thinking" with the flat statement that the Japanese take the phenomenal world as absolute. I shall return again and again to this theme, for it is a profoundly important characteristic of the contemporary Japanese world view. In the past, it proved to be powerful enough to effect the transformation of Buddhism itself into a religion almost wholly centered on this world.

Nevertheless, no people ever relied solely on pure pragmatism to see them through crises, and like others the Japanese have in the course of their history wrestled with momentous philosophical and ideological questions. Much of the material I have considered up to this point obviously falls squarely within the Confucian idiom. It is necessary at this juncture, then, to delve more deeply into the ways in which the Japanese have dealt with a problem posed by neo–Confucian thought: How shall the contradiction between history and the natural order be resolved? The resolution of the paradox of flux and constancy had far-reaching implications for the development of the modern Japanese state. Koschmann (1980) takes the works of the Mito scholar Aizawa Seishisai (1782–1863) to represent an instructive exemplification of Tokugawa thought on the issue. The problem is that the human agency must act in historical time, for it has no other dimension. It thus operates by devising expedients, the only techniques available to it. The paradox lies in this, that the ultimate purpose of action is universality and permanence. Aizawa wrestled with this issue throughout his career and his resolution of it could well have served as the motto for those who ultimately formed the new state. It was this: "The ultimate end of expedient and adaptive measures must always be the reconstitution of the universal order" (Koschmann 1980: 99). It will be remembered that it was the Mito scholars who provided the formulation that brought down the Tokugawa shogunate and paved the way for imperial restoration. It was Aizawa himself who, borrowing political priorities from the Confucian Analects, clothed them in the trappings of Japanese mytho-history and installed them as the foundation of *kokutai*, the national essence, which lies at the heart of both the Meiji Constitution and the Imperial Rescript on Education.

In their adoption of the formulation of the Mito scholars, the Meiji oligarchs embraced a doctrine of whose dangers they may not have been aware. For the neo-Confucian equation of natural law and the social order leaves open the way to two equally tenable interpretations of its implications for action: "Either by rigid adherence to pure doctrine it becomes a revolutionary principle directed against the concrete order, or by its complete identification with the actual social relations it becomes an ideology guaranteeing the permanence of the existing order" (Maruyama 1974: 199). Proponents of the two interpretations contended for power throughout the early Meiji period. The supporters of the popular rights movement argued that the state was a human invention. Thus, as the state is subordinate to humans, who have constructed it, it can be changed arbitrarily by human will. Those who opposed popular rights argued that the state developed in accordance with the natural character of humankind and thus was not a human product. States, then, were not subject to human control; humankind was subject to the control of the state. As Chang (1980:267) has remarked, at the core of the Confucian value system "was a belief in the substantial unity of the central values and norms of the existing social order with the structure of the cosmic order. This belief could generate tensions with the existing sociopolitical condition, but its more important effect was to freeze the normative order of state and society and render it absolute." Modern Japanese history offers ample testimony to the accuracy of Chang's comment, for until the end of the Greater East Asia War in 1945, the rulers of the Japanese state attempted to exercise control in the name of a restored cosmic order, fused in the person of the divine king.

That the attempt was even made is in many ways so astonishing that the discovery that Japan's leaders experienced increasing difficulty in maintaining control is hardly startling. What is intriguing, however, is the suggestion that the Meiji oligarchs had unwittingly created a revolutionary potential by denying the moral order as the Confucianists defined it and installing imperial will in its place. They may not have seen that they had created a society in which any person or group of any persuasion whatever might try to seize power with the claim of legitimation by imperial will. (There have even been calls for a socialist revolution under the guidance of the imperial family.) Perhaps they saw the danger but were not unduly concerned because at the outset they were so secure in their monopoly of the interpretation of that will. After the promulgation of the constitution, however, it was to become a major problem for the government, for the oligarchs had given imperial will a wholly arbitrary character; there was no natural political order (Silberman 1974: 443, 451).

Now it is all well and good to claim that we are dealing with a country whose polity was so recently defined in such cosmic terms, but the discussion so far shares with intellectual history the crippling weakness of failing to show how these ideas and attitudes were communicated by the rulers to the ruled, and to what effect. I propose to do just that by returning one last time to the Imperial Rescript on Education. The discussion has to do very directly with the sociology of religion, paradoxical as that may seem. The study of the sociology of religion in Japan is not much developed for two major reasons, of quite unequal weightiness. The first is that there really is nothing in Japan that corresponds to the Western concept of the church, a profound difference between the two systems that has far-reaching implications. The second and less weighty is doubtless an aspect of the Confucian heritage, for few Japanese intellectuals are at all interested in religion, with the result that the small number of social scientists who have engaged the problem are almost all Christians. I will focus on the absence of a distinction between church and state as more central to the matter at hand.

In 1891, the year following the promulgation of the Imperial Rescript on Education, a directive to all primary schools put out by the Ministry of Education declared the edict to be the foundation of moral education (*shūshin*). It was drafted by Inoue Kowashi, whom we have met before. He seems never to have intended the rescript to be used as it was, but recommended that it simply be directed to the Ministry of Education or read by the emperor as an address to the Peers' School or to the Association of Educators. Instead, it came to be worshipped as "a document of absolute infallibility" (Furukawa 1968:311–12). Perhaps both people and government share in the responsibility for this development, but our interest centers on the government, which did assign extraordinary importance to this document.

I do not know whether Inoue or any of the men around him

had read George Washington's Farewell Address, although in fact I consider it extremely likely that they had, for the heroes of the American Revolution early became their heroes as well. In any event, there is a passage in it that speaks clearly to one of their preoccupations:

And let us with caution indulge the supposition that morality can be maintained without religion. Whatever may be conceded to the influence of refined education on minds of peculiar structure, reason and experience both forbid us to expect that national morality can prevail in exclusion of religious principle.

Although it may well be that they had read Nakamura Keiu's (1832–91) translation of the address, they could easily have found these sentiments in any one of scores of Western books. Their interest in what these sources had to say on this issue can be attributed directly to their concern with constructing some kind of institutional context in which they could instill in the people their version of the new national morality. Their problem was that they had no church through which to accomplish their ends.

Buddhism, long since fragmented by sectarian disputes, could not serve. Moreover, there was a strong sentiment among the oligarchs, who were if anything Confucianists by persuasion, that Buddhism, far from providing an appropriate moral context, was both an alien (Indian or Chinese or Korean) religion and a corrupt exploiter of the common people. Yet in the West, they had found nothing but systems that posited an intimate and necessary connection between morality and religion. Their attempts to solve the problem were multifaceted, and in the early Meiji period took the form of the establishment of National Shinto as a state religion with its own system of shrines and priesthood, supervised from the capital. For a time, between 1869 and 1875, the promoters of the new state cult, whose high priest was the emperor of course, trained and sent out priests to propagate the new faith. Both Shinto and

Buddhist clergy were pressed into service, for the government
intended that as many teachers of religion and morals as
could be mustered were to spread the new morality of loyalty
to the emperor and the state. The effort was not necessarily
doomed, but strong protests from foreign governments over
the establishment of a state religion and continuing popular
support of the Buddhist rites finally led the government to
grant qualified religious freedom in the constitution of 1889.
Shinto had not become the kind of national religion its proponents had envisaged.[15]

As it happened, an alternative solution to the problem, to
find a way to instill the virtues of imperial loyalty and filial
piety in the people, was already in place. It was the national
system of compulsory education, established in 1872, where
the government had virtually a free hand. There being no
church, and the effort to construct one having failed, the Meiji
government simply moved the entire responsibility for training
in morality and ethics into the schoolroom. The aim of education increasingly became to produce loyal and obedient subjects, and the rescript of 1890 was made the basic sacred text
of the new religion of patriotism. The regulations subsequently
issued by the Ministry of Education defined the development
of moral character as the central mission of primary schooling
(Dore 1964:191).

The Confucian thrust is unmistakable. In the Analects,
there is a famous passage: "Their persons being cultivated,
their families were regulated. Their families being regulated,
their states were rightly governed. Their states being rightly
governed, the whole kingdom was made tranquil and happy."
If happiness was not the prime concern of the government,
tranquility certainly was. Since they believed a stable family
meant a stable society, the oligarchs took a bold step and as
if by a sleight of hand converted filial piety from a private duty
into a civic virtue. The conservatives found a way to weld the

imperial house to the people through the universally observed
practice of ancestor worship, which for centuries had been the
dominant mode of Japanese religious life, centered as it was
on the household rather than the temple. They effected this
union by the breathtakingly audacious utilization of a very old
idea, whose origins go back to the national mythology. They
reworked that idea and ended with the assertion that inasmuch
as all Japanese are descended from the imperial house, all are
related. The teacher's manuals, especially those issued after
1910, made the point explicitly:

> The connection between the Imperial House and its subjects is
> thus: one forms the main house and the others form the branch
> house, so that from ancient times we have worshipped the founder
> of the Imperial House and the heavenly gods. Our relationship to
> this house is sincerely founded on repaying our debt of gratitude
> to our ancestors. (Caiger 1968: 68)

And lest there should be any remaining, nagging doubt about
the conflation of imperial loyalty and filial piety, the subjects
of the emperor were said to be his children. The term used was
sekishi, literally "infants," and in that profound respect there
were no distinctions to be drawn among them. At the popular
level, this notion found support in established tradition of another kind entirely, for it is equally a tenet of Buddhism that
there is a fundamental equality among all beings who have not
yet broken the cycle of rebirth.[16] In their relationship to the
throne, therefore, all subjects are one, bound to it by genealogical ties and equally members of the family state.[17]

In their treatment of the institution of divine kingship in
archaic civilizations, Berger and Luckmann (1966:75) unwittingly offer an almost perfect summation of what the Meiji
oligarchs had wrought:

> ... [T]he symbolic universe provides a comprehensive integration
> of *all* discrete institutional processes. The entire society now makes
> sense. Particular institutions and roles are legitimated by locating

them in a comprehensively meaningful world. For example, the political order is legitimated by reference to a cosmic order of power and justice, and political roles are legitimated as representations of these cosmic principles.

It remains only to say that the system they constructed worked, perhaps all too well. Kurt Singer,[18] a German who taught in Japan from 1931 to 1939, wrote a poignant book about that society, filled with ambivalence and shadowed by the national debacle he lived to witness from afar. In it he pays the ultimate tribute to the sensibility with which I have tried to deal:

Modern states are more apt to disintegrate than the number and strength of unifying factors would suggest. A shared heritage of law, of education, of language and cult, of interests and animosities, may provide large nations with strong ligaments; but these cannot make up for the lack of [what the Japanese in the 1930s had], that feeling of unconditional connectedness.... (1973:75)

This should not be taken to mean that the modern history of Japan has been that of a tranquil society whose members think and act as one under the benign authority of a sacred monarch. To be sure, the Confucianists had labored mightily to elucidate the true relationship between ruler and subject and produced the concept *taigi-meibun*. The notion was that "subjects spontaneously performed the ethical duties appropriate to their subordinate positions" (Kinmonth 1981:84). Yet the most cursory survey of the record reveals a domestic political world far from harmonious, rendered pluralistic, contentious, and often perilous by the very granting of the constitution. Party politics of a seldom elevated description, corruption, and coups d'état, real and rumored, are part and parcel of political life from 1890 to the 1930s, the period when Japan's international stature grew in direct relation to its military successes against China and Russia and its participation in World War I on the side of the Allied Powers.

I have no wish to deny the importance of the turmoil and heterodoxy of the political and intellectual scene, nor do I intend to suggest that the forty-year period was unmarked by considerable social agitation and experimentation with what were soon to be denounced as "dangerous thoughts." Once again, however, I would remind the reader that while the politicians made and lost fortunes, died at the hands of assassins, and finally made possible the reaction disguised as restoration that ultimately rendered them irrelevant, the people of Japan for the most part went about their business.[19]

They lived under a civil code that determined the character of succession and inheritance in their households; they sent their children to primary school, where they were daily instructed in the duties of obedience, loyalty, filial piety, and the beauties of patriotic sacrifice. The young men were conscripted into the military forces and the young women employed in the expanding urban factory system, for it was the genius of the civil code that it required impartible inheritance and recommended primogenitoral succession to the headship of the house. All other children were thus spun off from the family into the factories or the military, and swelled the population of the cities. For Japan's farmers, laborers, and white-collar workers alike, except for an occasional outburst none of which can remotely be described as a popular uprising, the government disposed and the people acquiesced. They had little respect for politicians, who had scant grounds on which to claim it. The popular view of the bureaucracy was more sanguine, which is not to say that it was loved, for arrogant and imperious as the bureaucrats might be, they did seem generally to know what they were about.

By the late 1920s, however, forces within the military and elsewhere began to suggest that the times called for another restoration, for the glories of the Meiji era had begun to fade. It was to prove a restorationist movement of a very common kind. These men maintained that the original aims of the Meiji Restoration had not been—indeed, could never be—realized under a constitutional form of government.[20] The granting of a constitution had been a mistake, and only by restoring the direct flow of the imperial will to the people could those aims be achieved. The political parties, like the shogunate before them, would have to go, or at least be rendered impotent. It proved an easy task. In 1931 Japan moved into Manchuria; two plots aimed at restorationist military coups were uncovered; in 1932 the premier was assassinated. Alarmed by the prospect of growing disorder and terrorism, a group of senior statesmen and officials of the imperial court declared that henceforth the cabinets would be nonparty in character, so that national unity might once again be fostered. Few rallied to the defense of the political parties in 1932, and eight years later they were dissolved.

We are brought back to Kurt Singer, whose sojourn in Japan coincides almost exactly with the period from the Manchurian Incident to the creation of the one-party state. It was a troubled time, characterized by the growth of increasing chauvinism among the people. Much of that sentiment was fostered by the forces of reaction and xenophobia, but they were not very seriously opposed by the political left, which could always hope that allowing the excesses of the military and the right to run their course would serve to hasten the general collapse that must precede revolution. As Japan encountered mounting hostility in the world, and as the sense of isolation grew, the government's appeals for patriotic sacrifice grew more insistent and more strident. Not only the schools and the media, but village-level government itself was pressed into service to convey the message of the beauty of imperial loyalty, the need for ever greater sacrifice, and a sense that the Japanese, albeit uniquely united, were alone in the world.[21] The faith of the people was deep enough to propel them, with little dissent of any consequence, into one of history's great human catastrophes—with a sense of common kinship and a shared fate in the name of imperial loyalty and filial piety. It has been much debated in Japan whether soldiers cried out for their mothers or invoked the name of the emperor as they lay dying. To the writers of the Imperial Rescript on Education, the question would have seemed misplaced; had they not said that the two sentiments are identical?

In the chapters that follow, I will take up the question of what has happened in Japanese society during the generation since the end of the Greater East Asia War. In them I shall try to trace out the fate of the Confucian concept of order, the degree to which the feeling of unconditional connectedness has been affected, and the extent to which tradition continues to be created in the pursuit of societal goals.

2

Order and Diffuseness

"If there is a law governing this un-cosmic world of the
Japanese . . . it can only be a law of inescapable change
and universal impermanence."
Kurt Singer (1973:109)

In the preceding chapter I have made frequent reference to
the Confucian concepts of natural law and social order. That
emphasis stems from my conviction that the Confucian past
casts a very long shadow over contemporary Japanese society.
For all the exploitation of Shinto myth and legend by the
scholars of the School of National Learning,[1] and their importance in the formulation of the rationale for the overthrow of
the Tokugawa, it cannot be overlooked that for the 250 years
prior to the Meiji Restoration, the Tokugawa had ruled an
essentially Confucian state, with all that implies, among other
things, for the role of ritual and ceremony.

Masao Miyoshi has observed that ritual and ceremony are
expressions of the most essential values of the Japanese, and
that throughout the Tokugawa period they provided the
framework of unity of the society: "In the great chain of being
that—theoretically—connects the Emperor to the humblest
laborers via the Shogun, lords and myriad ranks of samurai,
farmers, artisans, and merchants, all must perform ceremony
so that order may be maintained throughout" (1979:87). The

37

"vision of the feudal order is firmly based on the theory of hierarchic distinctions. And as such it has a kind of holism involving the entire nation" (1979:198, fn 101).

Maruyama Masao points to the resultant character of the structure of that society and the locus of its values. Those who govern attempt to maintain the ordered unity of the total structure by linking its innumerable layers of closed, self-contained spheres. At the political level, such a system operates on the *principle of indirect control,* which means that "The right to establish and administer the law was allocated broadly to each status level. . . . To characterize this aspect of the feudal society in a phrase, we might call it a *hierarchic structure of immanent values.* The values of the total social system are diffused and embedded in each closed social sphere. As a result, each of these social spheres plays an indispensable part in the preservation of the total structure" (1974:243–4).

The conception of the social order has profound implications for the understanding of the nature of law in all countries. The Tokugawa legal system has long intrigued Western scholars, both for its contributions to contemporary Japanese law and for the peculiarity, as one of them has pointed out, that there is so little of it (Henderson 1968: 203–5). By and large the system did allocate to representatives of groups both complete authority and total responsibility for the performance and conduct of group members, based squarely on the principle of vicarious liability and collective responsibility. Thus, the taxes of a village were paid by its headman, who had the responsibility of collecting them himself. Domain law was never intended to deal with civil disputes in the village, which was expected to see to it that its residents behaved according to local custom and were properly cared for if in need. The firm requirement by the domain that the villages govern themselves may be primarily an acknowledgment of the limits of its power and the administrative weakness of the authorities

(Henderson 1975: 8–9, fn 37). Be that as it may, that is how the system worked, and because there was so little law, the system was only as effective and humane as the people who ran it (Henderson 1965: I,61).

These principles thus operated to assign a high degree of autonomy to village community and urban neighborhood alike. So effectively were they employed that in the 1850s and 1860s, for example, there were in Edo (now Tokyo) only 350 police officers, of whom 60 were responsible for dealing solely with members of the warrior class.[2] For the commoners of this great city of over a million people there were no police at all; the formation of a force was one of the first tasks of the new government, determined to be modern.

The concluding formulaic words of a typical document of the Tokugawa period state the principle of collective responsibility unambiguously: "If mistakes in the registers are found, or if there are any omissions from the registers, we admit the fault and will accept any kind of punishment. As proof and guarantee we hereby affix our seals and signatures" (R. J. Smith 1972:433). The document in question is signed and sealed by local civil authorities charged with ferreting out concealed Christians and other heretics who might be hiding in the area of their administrative responsibility. The penalty for harboring such persons, whether unwittingly or by design, was death. Although the language is archaic (the document is dated 1760), the sentiments of collective responsibility are by no means foreign to members of contemporary Japanese society, as I will attempt to show in this chapter.

If there is one word that subsumes much of what there is of Tokugawa law, it is conciliation. It is profoundly important in contemporary Japanese law as well—altered in the particular contexts in which it is employed, to be sure, but fundamental all the same. In the Tokugawa period the practice of conciliation sought agreement rather than legal determinations. Its aim was not to enforce legal rights, but to render highly specific justice, as determined subjectively by the parties to a dispute (Henderson 1965: I,180). Consequently, to the extent that conciliation agreements served as a substitute for decisions which otherwise would have comprised a body of judicial precedent, the law failed to develop principles of universal applicability. Therein lies a signal weakness in the system, of course, for conciliation does not provide the means "to enforce rights against power and authority. The question then becomes how to get justice against a petty tyrant or a corrupt official. The Tokugawa method was moral, just as it had been largely religious . . . in Western feudal society. But Japan lacked two concepts that were critically important to the Western transition . . . to modern constitutionalism: Confucian ethics had nothing like the Christian [concept of] individual equality before God; nor did it have a division of church and state" (1965: I,181).

Conciliation in three distinctive forms remains a cornerstone of the Japanese law (Henderson 1965: I,183–7). The first, essentially an informal discussion designed to lead to settlement, comes straight out of Tokugawa village practice. Called *jidan*, it differs from the older form primarily in that, in the event no settlement can be reached, either or both parties may today elect to pursue the matter in the courts. The second, called *chōtei*, is primarily a formal prelitigation procedure, and was devised piecemeal in Japan in the years between the two world wars. The third, *wakai*, is a direct German borrowing, a procedure by which the judge encourages and assists the disputants to reach a compromise settlement. Today, a very large but declining proportion of all civil disputes are settled by *jidan* and thus never come to trial. About 60 percent of all adversary cases filed in the courts are settled by one or the other of the two remaining forms of conciliation.

Something of the same style of dispute resolution even permeates the law of contracts. "The Japanese [tend to] regard a contract as a functioning relationship requiring mutual accommodation to future contingencies by the parties rather than . . . a written embodiment of strict rights and duties enforceable in court" (Henderson 1965: I,95). In this connection, it is significant that one of the least-used provisions of the 1890 Code of Civil Procedure was that of arbitration (*chūsai*), for the Japanese prefer to avoid any procedure that will have the effect of precipitating "the intervention of an outsider to settle a dispute at his discretion, rather than to facilitate mutual agreement" (ibid.).

If it is true that the Japanese avoid litigation where possible and resort instead to conciliation, and as I will show there are some who doubt that it is actually the case, why should it be so? The question forces us to consider an issue about which there is much contention and no little obfuscation—that of the extent to which harmony may be said to be a core value. The Japanese word is *wa*. Ōno Seiichirō provides us with an elegant definition: "Harmony consists in *not making* distinctions; if a distinction between good and bad can be made, then there *wa* does not exist."[3] Impatience with distinctions has a noble lineage in Japan. In the eighteenth century, Motoori Norinaga, a major figure in the School of National Learning, wrote:

The Way of the Gods does not contain a single argument that annoyingly evaluates things in terms of good and evil, right and wrong, like the Confucian and Buddhist Ways. It is opulent, big-hearted, and refined.[4]

Kawashima Takeyoshi has long been an eloquent spokesman for the view that it is the concern for harmony that lies at the heart of the avoidance of litigation, which is unacceptable in that it "presupposes and admits the existence of a dispute and leads to a decision which makes it clear who is right or wrong in accordance with standards that are independent of the wills of the disputants. Furthermore, judicial decisions emphasize the conflict between the parties, deprive them of participation in the settlement, and assign a moral fault, which can be avoided in a compromise solution" (1963: 43). It is important to avoid such clear-cut decisions, he suggests, because in Japan role definition is precarious. Inasmuch as each person's role is perceived to be contingent on that of others, the whole system is fundamentally incompatible with decisions based on fixed universalistic standards, such as are rendered in courts. Moreover, there is a feeling that if the alleged offender offers an apology for a deed, it is incumbent on the other party to show leniency (1963: 43–5). All students of Japanese court procedures have commented on the fact that the offer of a formal acknowledgment of fault and an apology for the act invariably results in more lenient treatment than would otherwise be indicated, as Paul McCartney quickly discovered after his arrest for attempting to enter Japan with a small quantity of marijuana in his luggage.[5]

Even judges have characteristically been reluctant to take the final step and attribute clear-cut victory and defeat to the two parties to a dispute, preferring to make a last-ditch effort at a compromise settlement. So well acquainted with judicial leniency is the Japanese public that as late as the 1960s, 98 percent of those accused of a crime and brought to court waived their right to trial by jury, from whose outcome it is only fair to say there is no right of appeal. Since the end of the Greater East Asia War there have been some changes in public attitudes. The more lenient judges have come under increasing fire, and parties to conciliation procedures of the *chōtei* variety have more and more tended to lodge the very nontraditional complaint that the mediator has paid insufficient attention to their rights under the law. What has scarcely changed at all is the per capita rate of litigation which, despite the universal belief that it has risen sharply, was actually lower in the mid-1970s than it had been in the mid-1960s.[6]

So much for the argument that there is a cultural or psychological predisposition on the part of the Japanese to avoid litigation. It clearly would be a mistake to overlook the structural constraints that as a matter of government policy have been created with the specific intent of minimizing the amount of litigious behavior. It is surely the case that disapproval of litigation is as much a part of the Christian heritage[7] as it is a Confucian legacy (Haley 1978: 389), which must force us to ask why there is so much more of it in societies of the former kind than in the latter. Haley has offered the trenchant explanation that Japan differs from other countries primarily in the successful implementation of policies that make it extremely difficult to litigate.

Certainly that has been the aim of government policy, which has kept the per capita number of judges and lawyers low. The ratio of judges to population declined from 1:21,926 in 1890 to 1:43,743 in 1982. In that same year, the ratio of all persons doing legal work, including many who are not called lawyers or attorneys (*bengoshi*), was 1:1,119, about twice that for the United States (Anonymous 1982). The courts are granted far less power to enforce their decisions than in almost any other industrial nation, and their severely crowded dockets produce long delays. All this lends credence to Haley's contention that the prevalence of conciliation is not merely the expression of a preference in Japan, but is the only recourse primarily because of the unavailability of effective mechanisms of law enforcement. Such evidence notwithstanding, most Japanese continue to believe that theirs is a nonlitigious society, and are persuaded that in a country where litigation is common, there is no morality.[8]

The explanations for the use of conciliation just given raise issues far more important than is suggested by the too narrow focus on the number of lawyers and judges or the powers of the courts. The question, of course, is whether the Japanese are by nature conciliatory and Japanese culture somehow inherently inimical to litigation. Nonlitigiousness should perhaps be taken as yet another of the long list of traits that make up the Japanese "national character." The position outlined above clearly is based on an emphatic denial of all three possibilities; it holds that the Japanese do not litigate because they are not permitted to do so. The implications of that assumption are manifold, but two seem to me to be particularly worthy of attention.

First, if there were more lawyers and judges, as there are in other industrialized countries, would Japanese rates of litigation rise to fill the available time and exhaust the available services of the legal profession and the judiciary? To respond affirmatively is to advance the dubious proposition that there must be some kind of universal human propensity to litigate, expression of which is uniquely denied the Japanese. The second assumption, equally unwarranted in my view, is that the Japanese government is endowed with an extraordinarily effective amount of skill or, alternatively, repressive power. Employing one or both, it alone of the governments of industrialized nations has contrived to fail to meet the (again, implied) desire of its people to abandon conciliation and resort to litigation. If this be so, then it is imperative to identify the sources of that awesome power. They are not readily apparent.

I do not believe that invoking "national character" or a reified "culture" will help explain or enable us to understand anything. Where, then, does this leave us? The alternative explanation need rely on neither state control nor national character. There is abundant evidence that in the conduct of their daily lives, the Japanese are at pains to avoid contention and confrontation. Reciprocity in human relations is a value taught to children from an early age, and much of the definition of a "good person" involves restraint in the expression of personal desires and opinions, empathy for the feelings and situation of others, and the practice of civility. Children are also taught that negative sanctions are likely to follow quickly upon behaviors that violate this value, which is reflected throughout the structure of interpersonal and social relations. In short, to focus on the law is to adopt far too narrow a frame. When the time comes in Japan that one takes pride in having pursued one's rights to the point of clear-cut victory over a forever defeated rival, when discrediting another becomes preferable to compromise that leaves both parties to a dispute with dignity intact, then the government of Japan will be unable to resist the pressures to unleash hordes of lawyers and judges who can satisfy these demands and create new ones. That day is still very far in the future, if it is to come at all.

It is clear that in Japan the use of law as guarantor of rights and duties is little resorted to directly. We must therefore ask if there is another mechanism that serves in its stead to reinforce and maintain the social order. There is, and it is to be found in the highly flexible and difficult to systematize domain of reciprocal obligations and human feelings called *giri-ninjō* (Y. Noda 1976:175–6). There are other kinds of obligations, to be sure, but it is these two words one hears most frequently in discussions of human relations. *Giri* is a duty or obligation of a person to behave in certain loosely prescribed ways toward another, to whom the person is indebted. The content and scale of the duty or obligation vary greatly according to the relative hierarchical positions of the two parties, the nature of the debt, and how it was incurred. Whatever the content or scale, however, the person to whom the obligation is owed has no right to demand that it be repaid; that is, such a person may specify neither the timing of the repayment nor its amount. Some return is expected, but should the person do anything but wait for voluntary repayment, that in itself would violate a fundamental premise of the relationship, for one's expectations must be tempered with compassion—*ninjō*. Nevertheless, the burden on the incurrer of the obligation is the heavier of the two, for if a conflict between *giri* and *ninjō* does arise, it is compassion that most often gives way.

Such relationships may be seen as perpetual, one repayment calling forth yet another expression of favor or consideration. In an earlier day the obligations transcended generational boundaries, continuing after the deaths of the persons who had initiated the relationship. Firmly embedded in the hierarchical order, the system is enforced by no formal sanctions—no one ever thought to take another to court to secure repayment of a debt of *giri*—but the person who violates the reciprocal relationship will be branded as without integrity or honor, and subjected to substantial informal sanctions.

The person who pursues the requirements of the code with care is universally admired. Let me offer one striking example of such behavior. In the course of a conversation with a Japanese friend one day, she happened to mention that a neighbor had dropped by recently to seek her advice on what kind of gift she ought to send a certain person. The neighbor, a widow in quite straitened circumstances, had just received a sum of money from the former geisha who had long been her husband's mistress. I registered my surprise and was instructed for the thousandth time in the niceties of *giri*. The woman's husband had always provided well for his family, but had also been quite generous to his mistress. Indeed, he had made it possible for her to buy out her contract and establish a beauty parlor, not an uncommon career for retired geisha, who are often set up in business by their patrons. Hers had prospered, and she felt that because she owed so much to this man, it was only fitting that she repay her debt to his widow. Said my friend, the people in that world—the demimonde of Japanese society that embraces geisha, teahouse proprietors, sumo wrestlers, kabuki actors, and performers of many traditional arts and crafts—are admirably sensitive to *giri*. The return gift, decided upon after much discussion, was delivered in person by the widow. It was a box of elegant confections from one of the city's famed traditional specialty shops, just the kind of thing, my friend said, that a former geisha would appreciate for its quality. There was a strong implication that the relationship between the two women would continue.

Like all codes of conduct in Japan, this one has a major component of relativity and flexibility, for its other face is human feelings or compassion. To be too rigid in the expectation of repayment is to violate the basic affective values that it is felt must ultimately govern human relationships. Such people—the overpunctilious on both sides of the interaction—are looked upon as being too "hard," their relationships with other human beings unleavened by warmth, understanding, or charity. The one who presses another to incur or repay an obligation will be accused of the serious failing of the obvious pursuit of self-interest: The system indifferently condemns both Uriah Heep and Ebenezer Scrooge.

Untempered by the compassion of *ninjō*, then, *giri* is conceived to be a monstrous burden. Sensitively employed, however, *giri-ninjō* blurs abstract hierarchy, permits subtle adjustment and concession, and assures continuity of relationships mutually satisfactory to their participants in an ever-shifting universe of calculable advantage and sacrifice. All are enmeshed in a web of obligations, and it is through the measured and considered response of all, as givers in some and receivers in other relationships, that the social order is in part maintained.

Nevertheless, it is a social order of a decidedly curious kind. I have posited the existence of a unifying hierarchical system within which role definition is contingent. The principle of harmony that admits of no distinction between good and bad, right and wrong, is plainly an aspect of what is often called situational morality, yet it is found to operate in a network of mutual obligation of a highly specific nature. In so diffuse a system, where could authority possibly lie? To the extent that the locus of authority appears to be problematic, one answer might be that we have got into a muddle, originating perhaps in a serious failure of definition or insufficient rigor of analysis. The only recourse is to examine each of the concepts in turn before attempting a synthesis—or at least arriving at some kind of compromise.

Most scholars who deal with Japanese society place at the center of their scheme of Japanese values something usually called a sense of hierarchy. Less thoroughly analyzed is this sense of hierarchy in action, a weakness that necessarily falsifies or obscures the treatment of social role. The study of the collection of documents from the Satsuma domain in the Tokugawa period to which I have already referred produced an extraordinary finding concerning the ranking system of the warrior class, and its complexities. It was found that rather than reflecting an abstract concept of the "lowness" or "highness" of a rank, the system accorded much more importance to the relative position of one rank vis-à-vis another and the obligation of each pertaining to the domain lord.[9] Upon closer inspection the ranking system proves to have a curiously diffuse character, in no small part because at the higher end of the scale ranking it was based on status differentiation, whereas at the lower end it reflected differentiation by function.

Well and good. We have long known that the Tokugawa conception of hierarchy was far more rigid in theory than in its practical application. Perhaps the same can be said of the sense of hierarchy in contemporary Japan. Many think so, and in support of their position point to the almost universal willingness to recognize that responsibility is collectively held and that any decision inevitably involves a number of people. Rodney Clark suggests a comparison that will on first reading seem to run counter to all we think we know about the Japanese and American societies. The idea of collective responsibility "is much easier to subscribe to in a Japanese company, with its relative homogeneity, its absence of extreme distinctions between management and labor . . . than it is likely to be in a Western company with its differentiated work force, sharp distinctions between management and labor, and dependence on specialized skills" (1979: 129). The assumption of collective responsibility for decisions and quality of performance, it need hardly be added, has far-reaching implications for the exercise of leadership, and much to do with the role definitions of leader and follower alike. The major implication of the diffuseness of hierarchy in Japanese groups is that the person who holds authority is no more or less autonomous than those over whom he theoretically wields power.

What, then, of role definition? Nakamura has made the famous remark that the Japanese always locate the individual in experience, not in the abstract.[10] A person is invariably identified as acting in some kind of human relationship, never autonomously. In this connection, as I will point out at greater length in the following chapter, we must confront the implications of a profound difference in linguistic usage between the Japanese and ourselves. In spoken as in written Japanese, the designation of the other—hearer and reader, as well as any third-party reference—precedes designation of the self. Put simply for present purposes, both self and other can be expressed only in relational terms.

The remaining issue, that of harmony (*wa*) is more recalcitrant. The principal source from which the ideology is drawn, and which itself partakes equally of the Confucian and Buddhist emphases on the overriding importance of social harmony, is the Seventeen Article Constitution of Prince Shōtoku, the great patron of Buddhism. Never mind that the document is surely later in origin than the traditional date of

A.D. 604, it occupies a central place in both official and popular literature on the concept. This first article, which opens with a direct quotation from the Confucian Analects, reads in part: Harmony is to be valued and an avoidance of wanton opposition to be honored.... [W]hen those above are harmonious and those below [well-disposed toward one another], and there is concord in the discussion of business, right views of things spontaneously gain acceptance. Then what is there which cannot be accomplished?" (Tsunoda et al. 1958: 50)

Although I am unaccustomed to citing *Sports Illustrated* in such contexts as this, let me recommend to the reader an article entitled "You've Gotta Have 'Wa'," which discusses some of the characteristics of Japanese baseball. More particularly, the piece deals with the impact of the concept of *wa* on American players who have been hired by Japanese teams. From this admirable essay, consider the following passage: "If you ask a Japanese manager what he considers the most important ingredient of a winning team, he would most likely answer, *wa*. If you ask him how to knock a team's *wa* awry, he'd probably say, 'Hire an American' " (Whiting 1979: 61).

It would be foolish to rest content with simply defining the term as something that they have and we do not, much as it is often suggested that the Japanese lack a sense of self as we understand it. We may turn for help instead to Rohlen's ethnography of a Japanese bank, whose company motto, For Harmony and Strength, provides the title of his book. First, he cautions, *wa* is not a metaphor, nor is it merely an element in a system of abstract distinctions. The word expresses a quality of human relationships, referring to "the cooperation, trust, sharing, warmth, morale, and hard work of efficient, pleasant, and purposeful fellowship. . . . [I]t is both a major means to social improvement and an end in itself" (1974: 47).

But we are talking about a bank here, and are thus led back to the issue of hierarchy. Like all large organizations, the bank is without any question hierarchically organized and so must somehow square that fact with the ideal of harmony and other principles of mundane social life. It does this, as is done throughout Japanese society, by emphasizing the small work group whose members are encouraged to "share a devotion to the success of the common effort and a respect for one another as partners in the enterprise. . . . In fact, it is the small group, not the overall company, that can actually be measured by the criteria of good relations presented in this ideology" of harmony (1974: 93–94). However often management may refer to the firm as one big happy family—and it does so with indefatigable insistence and frequency—what is far more important to the success of the whole is the degree to which its constituent small units approximate that ideal.

It seems appropriate, therefore, to turn to the small group in Japanese society for the light its analysis may shed on the apparent muddle of hierarchy, contingency, and harmony to which I have referred above. The generation of specialists in Japanese ethnology to which I belong conducted most of its early research in the village setting at a time when 70 to 80 percent of the population lived in rural areas. We concentrated on the village or hamlet and the household. One of the consequences of Japan's massive postwar urbanization has been a necessary shift of emphasis to research on the firm, the factory, the apartment complex, and the urban neighborhood as the units of study. I will try to confine myself to these more contemporary settings of Japanese society, particularly to the first two. Nonetheless, it is impossible to ignore the continuities between the household and these newer groupings.[11] Although I have no wish to be identified as yet another tiresome purveyor of the shopworn theme of the central place of "familism" in Japanese society, I feel constrained to indicate briefly where it seems to me the continuities lie. It is important to do so if only because in one crucial respect the nature of the

Japanese household has been so thoroughly misunderstood and misrepresented.

First, it should be noted that Japanese kin terminology is even more spare than that of contemporary American English insofar as it identifies particular statuses and specifies their attributes. To the extent that "kin terms are signs that guide behavior . . . Japanese usage alerts ego only to those closest kinsmen with whom he might, for household reasons, be expected to interact intensively, leaving behavior toward others to be prompted by other kinds of cues" (Pelzel 1970b: 228–9). Moreover, "Japanese theory has seen the household—and indeed any small face-to-face group—as internally all but unstructured save in terms of its leadership. . . . Guides to and limits on what it is proper to ask of a member of a . . . household of course exist, set superficially by age and sex attributes, and more deeply by what is understood of the experience and ability of the individuals. But most fundamentally they are set by the requirements of the group, and any member may legitimately be called upon to perform any action appropriate to the group's situation" (1970b: 244).

Once again we find diffuseness within what has long been taken to be a clearly hierarchical structure. But how could it be otherwise? Remember that the typical residential unit of the household was made up of a senior married couple and a married child with his or her spouse and their children. Such a unit could include as many generations as were alive, but there could be only one married couple in each generation. Among the vast agricultural, artisan, and commercial populations, the household was a corporate unit of production and consumption. Although it is true that in emergencies or peak seasons a household could depend on the assistance of other households, for most of the time and for most purposes it was an autonomous, self-sufficient unit. It follows that its members were obliged to perform multifaceted roles, for in terms of the size of its labor force it was very small—usually boasting no more than four able-bodied adults at any one time. Therefore, any person might be called on to perform any function of which he or she was capable, as I have noted, and it was the responsibility of the head of the household to take the leadership in the allocation of duties and responsibilities.

The head of the corporate household could enforce his wishes, it is true, in no small part because its internal system of roles presented so few cross-currents, as Pelzel has observed: "For some of the same reasons, he is constrained to be less arbitrary in the exercise of his authority. The head makes decisions, of course, as does his wife in her sphere of the domestic enterprise, but only after general discussion and consultation," for a decision not arrived at in this manner will not be carried through (1970b: 246). Thus the household is "institutionalized to express a variety of principles. . . . [T]hose expressing corporateness, hierarchy, solidarity, etc., we may wish to call 'formal' because they are cued to public patterns of behavior, or 'primary' because in any situation of conflict they have a clear priority. . . . [T]hose expressing collegiateness, *ninjō* (human feelings), and others, . . . we may wish to call 'informal' or 'secondary.' But the trick of successful group dynamics, and the mark of an able leader, is [the ability to act to] maximize the cultural demands to be satisfied in a given situation" (1970b: 248).

Indeed it is, and armed with this understanding of the Japanese household's structure, let us now consider the ways in which small face-to-face work groups operate in Japan. I do not believe for a minute that they are really like households, but all the evidence suggests that some of the principles outlined above apply to them very well. Rohlen says of the office group in the bank that the chief of a section has the power to make all decisions. Most of them nevertheless bring up issues for discussion by members of the group, and if they choose to do so may even apply the rule of consensus, usually on minor issues. On more major or urgent issues, they still consult with the entire staff, but tend to make the decisions themselves. Is there hypocrisy here? Rohlen (1974: 108) thinks not:

The conclusions may be foregone, but the fact that discussions have been held is most important, for a chief is expected to share his opinions, ask for advice, and permit dissenting voices [to be heard]. His trust and respect for the others and his acknowledgment of the group's importance, both symbolized by this [decision-making] process, are what counts.

One of the forms of consultation is the circulation of memoranda, planning documents, and policy drafts. Each person who reads them affixes a seal and may offer comments. "This system is so perplexing to Americans accustomed to a more dictatorial style of leadership from the top down that it has given rise to the myth that the Japanese have a mysterious bottom to top form of leadership called the *ringi* system" (Reischauer 1977: 188). Discussion of what seems to be taken for a uniquely Japanese invention frequently attributes to it a capacity for producing organizational control from below. The system is not mysterious at all, for the aim is simply to see to it that there has been extensive consultation within the group before a decision is made or announced. No matter how and by whom it is finally made, a decision preceded by this process deals with a problem with which all members of the group are familiar. They are therefore in a position to carry it out much more effectively than would be the case had the decision simply been announced (Reischauer 1977: 188).

At least one student of Japanese and American management practices maintains that the former do not actually use the participatory style any more than the latter. He did find, however, that communication was three times as likely to be initiated by people in lower management positions in the Japanese company than in the American. In his analysis he focuses not on the quality of decision making, but rather on the quality of the implementation of the decisions made. He quotes a senior executive of the Sony Corporation:

To be truthful, probably 60 percent of the decisions I make are my decisions. But I keep my intentions secret. In discussions with subordinates, I ask questions, pursue facts, and try to nudge them in my direction without disclosing my position. Sometimes I end up changing my position as the result of the dialogue. But whatever the outcome, they feel a part of the decision. Their involvement in the decision also increases their experience as managers. (Pascale 1978: 154)

Not only does the system permit dissenting voices to be heard, it allows the chief to capitalize on the experiences and abilities of the members of the section, much as I have suggested is the case in the household. In this connection, it is worth noting that Japanese firms tend to hire persons rather than to buy specific skills (that is, they induct cohorts of young workers upon graduation from school). It follows that the firm trains and retrains its workers and directs them where their talents seem most clearly to lie, but always in accordance with its long-range goals. The great seventeenth-century *haiku* poet Bashō taught different things to different people, perhaps "because he wanted to cultivate his pupils' talents rather than to impose his own theory upon them" (Ueda 1965: 36). Perhaps he was also following the Buddhist injunction to teach at the level that best fits the pupil. In modern Japanese industry, such training is thought to enhance the worth of the individual to the common enterprise by developing the person's capacities to the fullest.

In the early 1960s the quality control (QC) circle was introduced into Japan.[12] The circle is a small group of workers that meets on a regular basis to discuss aspects of the job, problems in the production process, and any other topic of

mutual concern. Their aim, of course, is to improve performance and increase productivity. At the outset, the foreman
served as leader of the circle. M. Noda (1980: 23) reports,
however, that some companies shifted to another system of
leadership selection by rotating the headship among all the
members of the QC circle in order "to bring the abilities of
all the participants into full play, to respect the personality
and concerns of each member, and to create a pleasant and
cheerful atmosphere for working and problem solving."

There is something perhaps too utopian in all this, for
there is surely another side to the matter: "To operate their
group system successfully, the Japanese have found it advisable
to avoid open confrontation.[13] Varying positions are not
sharply outlined and their differences analyzed and clarified.
. . . Much is suggested by indirection and . . . implication"
(Reischauer 1977: 135). True enough, but it would be unwise
to leave it at that, for in this context two additional considerations are in order. The first is handily disposed of by reference
to the frequently quoted Japanese proverb: The protruding
stake is hammered down (*Deru kui wa utareru*). Even in
intimate groups there are strong pressures to conformity,
which many have seen as the source of the deepest psychological malaise in Japanese society. In every situation there
comes a time when private predispositions and public requirements must be adjusted, and perhaps the highest tribute that
can be paid to the leader of a group is that he manages it so
that conformity and full participation in the group come to
be voluntary offerings made to the common enterprise (Rohlen 1974: 112). As for the effect of these constraints on the
individual members of the group, it is essential to understand
that

The cooperative, relativistic Japanese is not thought of as the
bland product of a social conditioning that has worn off all individualistic corners, but rather as the product of firm inner-self-control

that has made him master of his ... anti-social instincts. ...
[S]ocial conformity ... is no sign of weakness but rather the
proud, tempered product of inner strength. (Reischauer 1977: 152)

Confucius said of himself: "At fifteen I thought only of
study; at thirty I began playing my role; at forty I was sure of
myself; at fifty I was conscious of my position in the universe;
at sixty I was no longer argumentative; and now at seventy
I can follow my heart's desire without violating custom"
(Ware 1955: 25).

The second consideration of relevance to the analysis of the
decision-making process has to do with the manner in which
communication proceeds. I have already used the words "indirection" and "implication" to characterize it. The Japanese
"have a genuine mistrust of verbal skills, thinking that these
tend to show superficiality in contrast to inner, less articulate
feelings that are communicated by innuendo or by non-verbal
means" (Reischauer 1977: 136). This means that many mes-
sages are not only minimal but actually obscure as well, so
that the success of communication depends as much on the
sensitivity of its recipient as on the quality of the message
sent. Indeed, failure of communication, which is not uncommon, is generally blamed on the receiver. It follows, therefore,
that the more experiences sender and receiver have shared in
repeated encounters, the greater the likelihood of successful
communication. It may plausibly be argued that certain Japanese social values can be interpreted either as efforts to increase
the probability of success in communication, or as results of
its frequent failure.

So it is of no little interest to discover that employees of
a firm spend a great deal of time together off the job, far more
than is the case in the United States,[14] and to the extent that
they build up a long, intimate association there is a greater
chance that communication, however indirect, will prove
effective. Indeed, this style is valued over alternative modes;

sending too clear a message implies that the sender has a low regard for the sensibilities of the receiver (Nagashima 1973: 95). A person who habitually argues with logical consistency is regarded as immature and may earn the label that is one of the most wryly pejorative terms in the Japanese lexicon— *rikutsuppoi*, in Keifer's (1976: 281) indispensable translation, a "reason-freak." All members of a group expect their unstated feelings to be understood and their unarticulated desires to be anticipated. A husband can make no more cutting remark about his wife than that he is always obliged to ask for what she should have sensed he wants.

This line of argument has been carried even further. "If the limited . . . group is the structural foundation of society in Japan, an extremely pragmatic spirit acts as the mainspring of its dynamics. This seems perfectly reasonable among a people who eschew universal principles and act for the most part without superimposing a conceptual framework on the world" (Maraini 1975: 70). Almost thirty years ago, Ronald Dore (1958: 88) addressed this issue in his study of the residents of a neighborhood in Tokyo, buffeted by the new values and premises that had swept in after the Greater East Asia War over the rubble of the old and now discredited ones. Summarizing his findings on attitudes toward a great variety of issues, findings that had revealed no neat break between the traditionalists on the one hand and the modernists on the other, he wrote:

The changes in attitudes and behavior which are taking place are often discrete and unrelated to each other—unrelated both in the sense that they have different immediate causes, and in the sense that they are not related in the minds of the people who experience them. They are, moreover, taking place gradually; some are already thoroughly assimilated . . . , others . . . have only just begun.

What I have called the process of incorporation of the flood of postwar values was then far from complete. That process has not been completed today.

Twenty years later, Rohlen (1974: 60, fn 12) commented on the implication of this and many similar findings:

Western observers, including myself, find reason to be amazed at the Japanese tolerance for contradictory and even ludicrous explanation and meaning given by authorities to daily social patterns. We feel that each individual should examine, personally decide on, and remain consistent with a set of coherent and logical principles, and when the Japanese do not emphasize these things, we are likely to seek explanations in terms of some concept like the undeveloped sense of self. This, however, tells us more about our own understanding of self and personhood than it tells us about the Japanese. The fact remains that in the Japanese company world doctrinal strife is not at all common, and the possible social science explanations for this are numerous and generally unsatisfactory.

Now to many of my social science colleagues this kind of talk is anathema, said to be typical of a mushy, romantic obscurationism they deplore. It is characteristic of what one of them calls the "gee, whiz!" school of anthropology. It is with some relief, therefore, that I am able to turn to the results of some recent research by Robert Cole (1979: 250), one of the group of sturdy nonsentimentalists who has studied labor–management relations in Japanese industry. He is not concerned directly with the possible incompatibility of the several contradictory views that an individual seems to be able to entertain without conflict. But he is deeply interested in the interaction of the values and attitudes carried forward from the past and those more recently arrived on the industrial scene. It is further his concern to see how the old and new fit together insofar as they provide motivation for behavior. He finds the social locus of their harmonious fusion in precisely the context we have already identified—the small work group.

He comes at the issue from a typically no-nonsense position. What, he asks, has produced such a high degree of dependency of subordinates (workers) on superiors (management) in contemporary Japanese industry? He believes the answer to lie in "the heritage of values, ideology, and past practices which are brought to bear as constraints on current choices." The managers have succeeded so well because they "have had available a coherent set of preindustrial values and practices that could be mobilized to provide the ideological justification for the dependency relationships." He does not add what is self-evident, that the workers fully share these values. Yet, despite the essentially negative loading he assigns the high degree of dependency, Cole is struck, as any American must be, by the equally high degree of dependability displayed by workers, who actually appear to see themselves as full-fledged members of the organizations by which they are employed. To be sure, their dependability is encouraged by good wages and constantly improving working conditions, but these alone are not enough. There must be something more to it than that; there is, and it is to be found in the character of the primary work group. For it is here that workers develop a sense that they are participants in the enterprise and exercise influence on the organization.

At the heart of the system, then, he finds "a fundamental humaneness about the mode of organizing people. Individuals belong and they have goals that give clear-cut direction to their lives." The distinctiveness of the system, in which QC circles have enjoyed an explosive popularity, lies in its largely successful attempt to maximize the harmonization of individual and organizational goals. Among male salaried and wage workers alike in larger firms, he finds minimal alienation squarely in the context of tight control by management (1979:252–3). No one pretends that the system of participation of workers is democratic.[15]

In recent years many Japanese firms have set up operations in the United States, producing a large number of plants in which the management is Japanese, the work force American.

One of these is the Auburn Steel Company in Auburn, New York (Omicinski 1981). The application of Japanese management practices has produced a result that might well be pondered by those Americans who still believe their compatriots would, if given the choice, express a preference for rugged individualism over groupism of any description. In the interviews conducted with this group of workers about their reactions to the plant as a place of employment, one favorable comment is made again and again—the Auburn Steel Company has a "family atmosphere." One worker who had quit his job at a huge steel plant in California attributed the family character of the Auburn facility to the absence of a union (in 1977 the United Steel Workers' bid to organize the plant was overwhelmingly defeated by 82 percent of the employees). These people endorse the team concept of work: "It's a better atmosphere with a small group of guys. What we do is our accomplishment," said one, and another volunteered that he is well taken care of—"It feels like family."

Surely the most outstanding result of the utilization of the strength of primary group affiliation in Japanese industry is the negligible erosion of the Japanese work ethic. Reischauer (1977: 154–5) is impressed, as are most foreign observers, by the intensity of the individual's identification with the work group and the "enthusiastic, even joyous, participation in its activities. . . ." But it is upon the holder of authority within each small group that the heaviest responsibility lies, just as it falls on the shoulders of the household head. If the system is to work well, what kind of person should that be? Since 1953, the Japanese government has been conducting a survey of what it calls *kokuminsei*, "national character." One of the questions has to do with the kind of boss or supervisor one would most like to work for, and the responses to it have scarcely changed over the years.

The two kinds of boss are described as follows: The first is a man who always follows the rules and never orders his subordinates to do anything unreasonable, but who takes no interest in their personal affairs which have nothing to do with the work situation. The second is a man who sometimes requires his subordinates to do jobs beyond those specified by the regulations, but who takes an interest in the personal lives of his subordinates. The choice consistently favored by about 85 percent of the respondents is the second—the boss whose behavior toward his subordinates is replete with *ninjō* (Hayashi 1976). This word, as I have already pointed out, has a very broad meaning, and the frequent rendering "paternalism" is far off the mark. "Sympathy," "understanding", and "humaneness" are more satisfactory words that come to mind. A domineering, autocratic superior may be obeyed for want of alternatives, but the superior who is understanding and sensitive to the feelings of others in this broad sense is the person for whom one gives all of which one is capable. It is such a person, adept at the direction of the decision-making process, who engages in careful and extensive consultation in the course of which, at the very least, all opinions are heard before the final decision is made. The bottom line is not merely the productivity figures or even the balance of profit; there is another calculation to be made and that is the quality of the human relationships that are developed in the course of getting the job done (Pascale 1978: 161–2).

Only a few years ago it would have been easy enough to assume that these kinds of groups and leaders were merely one more aspect of the passing scene in Japan, part of the feudal residue of an unhappy time. Today that position is no longer tenable. Convergence theorists will no doubt find little comfort in the following item, which appeared in a publication (Anonymous 1981) put out by the employees of my university in 1981, just two months after the service and maintenance personnel had voted in the union:

Mini-Management Course
The New Style in Leadership

Business and social groups are getting an increasing share of
new-style leadership. These trained leaders are displacing the
old-style, who elbowed their way up by "doing what came naturally" in handling people. This comparative listing shows some of
the basic differences in the two styles.

Old-Style Bosses (*Autocratic*)	*New-Style Leaders* (*Democratic*)
Knew it all; made own decisions then pushed to make the decisions workable.	Feels his or her way. Asks questions; gets help from those concerned as decisions are reached.
Talked aggressively. Tried to get people to follow by talking or arguing them into it.	Brief in talking. Listens to learn what others think, or know, or feel, and leads through their own ideas.
Felt that good pay for an honest day's work was enough for anyone.	Adds a "mental wage" of congenial work groups and a feeling of being appreciated.
Kept others in the dark about future plans or proposed changes. Did the planning alone. "I"	Keeps members of social or work group up to date on what may be in store; often works out plans with them. "We"
Tried to control others by having strict rules and giving orders. Discipline and penalties.	Not much dependence on rules and penalties; more freedom of discussion to bring out the best in others.
Kept his distance so they would have respect and obey when the boss spoke.	Acts as human as the next one. Closer to the group and they follow the leader for other reasons than his or her authority or wealth.

Policy of finding fault on theory they would work harder, or not ask for a raise. Put on pressure.	More use of encouragement and helping others solve their business and social problems. Eases frustrations.
Felt that the attitudes, ideals, goals he or she told them to have were what they should have.	Realizes such thinking is picked up from work crews and other groups they belong to, so leads through these rather than by "preaching."
Acted on theory that success of an undertaking depended on the judgment and hard work of a few gifted people (such as me). "My goal"	Methods based on belief an organization succeeds by teamwork, people pulling together all up and down the line. "Our goal"

The new-style leader described in this fascinating document is by now familiar to those who have followed me this far. Convergence occurs after all, but it may take unexpected directions.

Nonetheless, it was generally held until fairly recently that the Japanese could not continue to count on workers to behave in a manner that surely was anachronistic, even feudal. The strong identification with the work group and its leaders of *ninjō* would, it was claimed, be swept away by the rising tide of independent-minded young workers entering the labor force. It was natural enough to imagine that it would be so, given the immense shifts in Japanese society that had so fundamentally shaken the structure of the corporate household and left in the rural areas only a shadowy remnant of the corporate village.

Now it would appear that the reverse has happened, for we have been considering what turn out to be relatively new styles of group commitment. The QC circle movement began only in the early 1960s, as we have seen, and the famed lifetime commitment of employer and employee in the large-scale industries, and not a few of the smaller ones, has assumed its now classic shape only in recent decades.[16] It seems, in fact, that both the degree of dependency of subordinates on superiors and the pressure to conform to group norms have increased in direct proportion to the collapse of traditional hierarchies: "Ironically, it is in the post-war period, when many of the values of dependency were, at least on the surface, being rejected, that we see a greater acceptance by employees of dependency relationships. To be specific, structurally based dependency grew at the expense of personally based [hierarchical] dependency relationships" (Cole 1979: 248).[17] Furthermore, Japanese studies of worker morale have repeatedly shown that it is positively correlated with size of firm. The larger the corporation, the less employees are constrained by the sense of being subject to an overbearing hierarchy above them. Moreover, since there is a marked tendency in Japan to form larger and larger organizations, it seems reasonable to expect that throughout the system worker morale will tend to rise. It is in the small firm, with the clearest personally based hierarchical relationships, that we find morale to be the lowest (Azumi and McMillan 1976: 223,226).

It is also in the larger companies and manufacturing enterprises that the pattern of after-hours association among workers is most firmly established (Atsumi 1979). Called *tsukiai,* it involves some four or five hours of socializing with other employees every day after work. The group may go to a bar or two, then to a restaurant, and finally to a coffee shop or another bar. The interurban commuter trains are full of these men making their way home from about nine or ten in the evening. They often arrive long after the children are asleep, and seldom eat at home except on weekends. It is because of *tsukiai* that salaried husbands and fathers are sometimes referred to as "week-end guests."

The reasons for the importance assigned this associational

pattern in larger firms are not far to seek. In a small company it is not difficult to know one's co-workers well, but in larger ones personal contact on the job is more likely to be restricted. Given that limitation and the highly unspecific nature of job descriptions, it is incumbent on those whose diffuse authority is exercised up and down the line to get to know the problems and preferences of those with whom they may have to interact during the working day. They can size one another up, cement informal relationships of trust and respect, learn who cannot be counted on, and establish their own credentials. But we must guard against making the easy assumption that *tsukiai* relationships are friendships. This common misinterpretation is made by Western observers, I suspect, because the public in Japan is so open and the private so closed. *Tsukiai* is, in fact, a major aspect of the person's work relationships, while one's friends are a much smaller group of former classmates and participants in common interest association (Atsumi 1979:65).

It is no exaggeration to say that *tsukiai* is an indispensable technique designed to make affairs of the firm run more smoothly, and that the larger the enterprise, the more necessary it becomes. This phenomenon is not a simple transfer into modern corporatism of an established tradition; like the QC circles and the lifetime commitment, it too is a new device that meets new needs of industrial society as the Japanese perceive it. To the Japanese, it appears that their industrial society runs more effectively and more productively in part because they draw a clear line between its requirements and their personal preferences, giving priority to the former. Many would, in fact, prefer to spend less time with their co-workers off the job, but there are formidable pressures to make them do so.

So well established is the notion that a man's career is in part determined by the skill and intensity of his use of *tsukiai* that his family may worry if he comes home from work early on weekdays. The wife of a recently married former student of mine once asked me if I had heard anything that might indicate he was not doing well at his university, where he had recently gotten a job. I told her I thought he was well regarded and asked why she was concerned. "He comes home for dinner every night," she said. "It must mean he's having trouble at work." She was unconvinced by my guess that he simply preferred not to drink with his colleagues and instead spend his time with his new bride.

The growth in size of firms has been accompanied by increasing commitment to the work group as well as acceptance by employees of new kinds of dependency relationships of a structural kind. If these are outcomes of the recent period of Japanese economic expansion, they surely contradict the expectations of many. Further, they suggest the emergence of a relationship between society and self that few would have predicted thirty-five years ago. We have come, then, to a question that has long preoccupied both Japanese and foreign observers alike. Japan is, after all, a modern industrial state, almost totally urbanized and successfully competing in world markets against its erstwhile mentors. If that society really is ordered on the principles I have outlined, where can the sense of self possibly lie? Can the Japanese individual be so completely submerged in the group that there is no room whatever for the development of the sense of self and the definition of personal identity? It is on that question that I will focus in the following chapter.

3

Self and Other

Studying as a child, studying as a student, studying as an official,
studying abroad; it was all just an act. However much I longed
to wash this painted face of mine, come off the stage for a
moment, and think about myself in peace; however much I
hoped to catch a glimpse of the face of that something behind,
I just continued performing role after role, the director's
whip at my back.
(*Mori Ōgai at the age of 49, in Mōsō* [*Day Dreams*];
Bowring 1979: 256–7)

We have now seen something of the nature of the small group
in Japanese society and explored some of the principles that
characterize its operations, but I have said little of the individuals who comprise these groups. Let me begin by citing some
very harsh judgments made of the Japanese by themselves and
others.

Masao Miyoshi, a scholar of English literature long resident
in the United States, writes about the emergence of the novel
after the Meiji Restoration: "The Japanese *Bildungsroman* is
not so much about the self's discovery of the self, as about the
self's discipline of itself into a productive model hierarchically
classified and blueprinted in detail by society at large" (1974:
xi). Attempting to explain what he regards as the failure of
the form in Japan, he observes that in the West the novel
"always pulls toward freeing people from their role character-

68

istics, and it is against such energy that Japanese society works so relentlessly with its tribalism and ceremonialism. . . . Novelists need people [and] the problem for the Japanese novelist is that there is no general acknowledgment in his culture that noticeable personalities should be allowed to exist" (1974: 80). There is a "poverty of real content in Japanese life; the novel . . . demands more richness and variety in experience than is normally supplied the writer in Japan" (1974: 170).

Kurt Singer, writing after the Greater East Asia War about the Japan he had known in the interwar years, is perhaps less harsh but undeniably more chilling: "The Japanese are difficult to understand, not becuse they are complicated or strange, but because they are so simple." By simplicity, he does not mean the absence of a multiplicity of elements. Quite the contrary: "The cause of what strikes us as alien and impenetrable in Japanese minds is not the presence of a bewildering array of conflicting elements in their psyche, but rather the fact that no conflict is felt to exist [among] them." There follows a series of aphorisms, which I have gleaned from the text: Conflicts are not fought out; they are eschewed. Life means surrender, not fulfillment. Creation is replaced by juxtaposition; synthesis by swiftness of transition (1973: 47–51).

In 1961 Arthur Koestler published a book about India and Japan called *The Lotus and the Robot*, which unintentionally celebrates the failure of the quintessential European intellectual to be broadened by travel. In it he describes the Japanese as possessing a "tolerance devoid of charity," and finds them to be a nation of "stoic hedonists, of Spartan sybarites." Charging them finally with a failing in which he himself clearly shares, he writes: "Unable to achieve a synthesis, they rejected compromise, and settled for the juxtaposition of extremes" (1961: 274, 206).[1]

Christie Kiefer (1976:280–1) is both more cautious and more sensible:

Compared with Western urbanites, Japanese tend to be more particularistic and situational, sociocentric, and feeling-oriented. Particularism and situationality refer to the tendency of the Japanese to alter their perceptions and values according to the immediate social demands of the situation. . . . Truth and morality are socially constituted; they are specific to the interaction at hand. . . . Sociocentrism is [a tendency] to prefer relationships that are binding, stable, and all-encompassing to those that are contracted and dissolved on the basis of specific utility. . . . Although Japanese are often acutely aware of discrepancies . . . between inner feelings and outward role demands, they think of the latter . . . as the really important center of the self. Regarding feelings as highly idiosyncratic and hard to control, and therefore less reliable as sources of self-respect than statuses and roles, the Japanese tends to include within the boundaries of his concept of self much of the quality of the intimate social groups of which the individual is a member. In contrast, the urban American self-concept is apt to stop at the skin.

Turning to the theme of alienation of the individual in contemporary Japanese cities, he cites a short story by Yamakawa Masao entitled *The Talisman* (1976: 298). It concerns a young resident of a large apartment complex who, "so depersonalized that he begins to doubt his own independent existence, carries a stick of dynamite around in his briefcase in order to convince himself of the possibility of having some impact on his surroundings."

Perhaps the largest single body of work on Japanese character and personality is that produced by George DeVos.[2] Although it is difficult to do justice to all the complexities of his position, it may be outlined briefly as follows. The personality of the individual is essentially completely formed during the process of early childhood socialization within the family. There the child is given unlimited gratification by the mother, instilling in it formidable dependency needs. Parents, but especially mothers, teach the child that it has the power to hurt them grievously by failing to live up to their hopes for it, or by falling short in its efforts to discharge the unrepayable debt it owes them in return for their suffering and sacrifice. Thus the dependency needs of the child are manipulated in order to generate high achievement needs. Because the child soon realizes that it can never in fact fully repay its debt to the parents, the adult goes through life saddled with an enormous burden of guilt. At the same time, the child's aggressive impulses are stifled from infancy, and the individual thus avoids aggression throughout life.

This process of socialization produces a self that is not independent of the attitudes and expectations of others, making the individual highly sensitive to insult or slight. The pressing need for personal accomplishment, which by definition will never be great enough, causes the adult individual to invest a high degree of identification with and involvement in whatever role he or she is playing. Japanese achievement motivation, which is very high, is based not on training for independence and self-reliance as in the West, but rather on the instilling of affiliative and dependency needs. The experiences of adult life are dealt with in terms of a personality set through early childhood socialization which, because no other explanation is offered in this paradigm, alone shapes the personality of the adult. It is not a particularly appealing picture.

William Caudill (1972) has further suggested that the Japanese preference for acknowledgment of interdependence over expression of independence may be established as early as the first months of life. Observation of the character of interaction—feeding, holding, talking—between mother and her newborn infant suggests that the psychological boundaries between the two are indistinct. That is, the baby is felt to be an extension of the mother rather than an autonomous being, as is the perception in the United States. This pattern of interpersonal dependency extends throughout the person's adult life. As many people have pointed out, a little later in life the child learns a harsh reinforcing lesson. In Japan an obstreperous child who cannot be controlled may be punished by being put outside the house, to be readmitted only when it has calmed down. In the United States, being kept in the house or in one's room is (or was) the punishment for analogous behavior. The contrast is taken to express a marked difference in the degree to which the child's identification with the family is fostered, and a major component of the Japanese adult's fear of being ostracized from any group of which he or she is a member.

On the other side of the debate are other voices, including that of the irrepressible Fosco Maraini (1975: 48–9), who registers a violent objection to the overwhelming priority assigned by DeVos and others to family-induced guilt in the creation of high achievement motivation in the Japanese personality. It is so fierce as to be worth quoting at length:

... in the center of [the theoretical picture] stands (or sits, or squats) the family, a carnal and emotional alcove cum laboratory, where formidable tensions build up in secret and are stored away in the younger individual members [in] the form of guilt—only to be released later [to power] the ... engines of motivation leading to achievement.... The entire picture is grim and gloomy, dismal and fierce. Readers lacking direct knowledge of the Japanese will probably imagine them as tortured dwarfs perennially on edge, as nervous and irritable hypochondriacs, with their embers of guilt burning inside them, marching uncomfortably ... to the consummation of ugly compulsive destinies.

Maraini finds them instead to be good humored and kindly, possessing extraordinary psychological poise, exhibiting an intensity of pleasure and an eagerness in action. Besides, as Pelzel (1970a: 55) mildly cautions us to remember, "It is surely as much the habit of modern Japanese as it was that of their ancestors . . . to engage for the most part in proper acts, impelled thereto by positive sanctions. . . ."

Others are equally persuaded that the entire matter of the Japanese character and its development has been vastly over-simplified. Among them, David Plath has offered a view of the adult life course in Japan that helps us understand how they define and attain maturity. In the West we are taught the central importance of nourishing and developing our individuality. Social conformity is defined as a positive evil when carried beyond a very low threshold of behavior. It is hardly surprising that foreign observers find the Japanese to be collectivity-oriented, too likely to submerge the self in the group, and possessed of weak ego boundaries that are all to permeable. In short, we find that the Japanese are apparently willing to forego growth as individual human beings, and lack the kind of self-reliance we deem essential to self-realization. What this view causes us to miss is that the Japanese assign a high priority to the growth of human beings as social persons. The picture that we have of them fails "to take account of the expanding awareness of the world and the self, the ripening capacity to care for others in their terms, the increasing ability to apply one's own experience, that are hallmarks of the mature person in Japan as elsewhere" (1980:4).

Although conceding that Japanese values may indeed assign general priority to group over self, Plath rightly insists that individual values are also prized, so long as these do not lead to nihilistic self-centeredness or selfishness. Thus, there can be a complementary relationship between group and individual values, "For the Japanese view is that only from . . . a corporate group can one be assured of getting sensitive responses to one's human needs—a guarantee of one's personal integrity. . . . The interactionist self . . . emerges—or is enacted—in social relations. Awareness [of self] . . . is endlessly re-created as one lives on, responding to the responses of others" (1975: 3–5). It is for these reasons that the Japanese stress refinement, circumspection, sensitivity, and even compulsiveness in their efforts to create pleasant social relationships (Lebra 1976: 6), for the goal of interaction is interlocking and fusion of persons rather than confrontation between them.

Forced to choose between the two points of view respecting Japanese personality, character, individuality, personhood, sense of self, and the rest, I would have to opt for the latter. It is not mere idle speculation to suggest that our understanding of these matters would be very different today if over the past thirty-five years research had been conducted in the framework of the interactionist social psychology of figures like George Herbert Mead (Strauss 1956) and Henry Stack Sullivan (Perry and Gawel 1953), rather than the individual psychology of Freud and others who provided the framework that was in fact employed. Had the intellectual influences been different, we should long since have had an eminently plausible picture of the Japanese conception of the self.

It would have been an interactionist self. In support of that flat statement, I should like to consider two absolutely fundamental characteristics of the Japanese language. The first is the phenomenon of *keigo*, variously translated "honorific language," "polite speech," or "respect language." *Keigo* has to do with the expression of status differences, politeness, deference, and intimacy. The second, and closely related, characteristic of the language is the absence in Japanese of anything remotely resembling the personal pronoun. Let us agree for the moment that both phenomena may well have something to do with the conception of the self held by speakers of the language.

In the context of any given communicative event in Japanese, *keigo* has the effect of establishing at the outset the relative social standing and degree of intimacy of the speaker, the listener, and any third-party referent. Japanese is very poor in vocabulary that is neutral with respect to status differences, and what there is is found in its most fully developed form, Miyoshi (1974: xiii–xvi) has argued, in the post–Meiji novel.

The divergence between spoken and written Japanese, still very great today, was immense at the beginning of the Meiji era. The written language was refined but too remote; the spoken was familiar but too vulgar to suit the purposes of art. The novelists of the time, faced with a dilemma and unable to choose between the alternatives, worked out a compromise. They wrote a "sort of dignified colloquialism" by means of which they could establish a level of speech for the novelist-as-narrator that would neither offend nor overly exalt the reader. Adoption of this "neutral level, neither deferential nor condescending . . . solved some problems but . . . introduced others. For the 'neutral' level has no counterpart in conversational usage; it is strictly an artificial language, for use in fiction alone. . . ."

There are occasions in daily life, nevertheless, when one interacts with at least a near-equal, and it is instructive to see how these relatively rare situations are handled. In such interaction "between young male equals, each speaks as though the listener were his inferior [that is, both use less polite speech]; between female equals, each speaks as though the listener were her superior [that is, both use more polite speech]; between male and female equals, she speaks with [deference], he without it . . ." (Miyoshi 1974: 13). In short, even where status differentiation is weakly marked, lacking access to a truly neutral vocabulary, the speakers are obliged to determine which of the status-sensitive vocabularies to employ.

The problem faced by the Meiji novelist as narrator, that of establishing a position relative to the reader, is one that today bedevils advertising copywriters. They would like their copy to avoid condescension and express deference, while at the same time moving readers or hearers to purchase the product. The problem is that the use of the imperative mood in Japanese is strictly limited to commands to a subordinate or orders to a social inferior. It being thus quite out of the question simply

to urge an audience to "Drink Coca Cola!" or "Buy Japanese!"
or "Eat!" writers resort to a number of evasive circumlocutions
or, more interestingly for our purposes, rely on exploitation of
a particular kind of status incongruity. The television viewer is
commanded to drink, buy, or eat—all in the imperative—by
ingratiating comedians, coquettish women, and coy children,
all nonthreatening figures of low status (Higa 1972:53),
chosen as much for their appealing vulnerability as for their
neutrality. There is quite literally something of a "Smile when
you say that!" quality about the way in which their commands are delivered. At least one aspect of this technique is
not new. In the classic *nō* drama as it is still performed today,
the roles of emperors are taken by little boys, except where the
emperor portrayed is Chinese and no question of *lèse majesté*
arises.

Television affords yet another example of the working out
of the problem of status differentials. There are probably few
countries in the world where the opinions of authorities, real
or imagined, are so avidly sought for dissemination to an
eager audience. Professors, authors, bureaucrats, physicians,
professionals and specialists of all kinds, even foreigners who
happen to speak Japanese passably well, are brought into television studios and handsomely paid to express their views on
a truly staggering array of topics. Almost invariably the format
of these appearances is the same. Accompanying the person of
authority is a young woman, or far less likely a young man,
whose sole function is summed up by the name of the role—
kikite, the listener. The author or university professor, male or
female, clearly occupies a higher status than that of the *kikite*,
to whom opinions are expressed, recommendations made, insights offered, and the meaning of complex and difficult issues
made clear. By means of this device, the whole troublesome
matter of the selection of proper speech levels is handily resolved. The speaker addresses the younger person rather than

the viewing audience, presumably a body of a highly hetero-geneous nature, and thus avoids giving offense by adopting too lofty a tone, or equally lethal, presuming too great familiarity. For her part, the *kikite* uses extremely polite language in addressing the audience directly, for she is in a position relative to them of a purveyor of services.

It is impossible to speak or write Japanese without employing *keigo*. The level chosen by each speaker, who is compelled to make a choice before uttering a verb form, is based on calculation of social distance, largely conceived in terms of a complex combination of age, sex, social position, nature of previous interactions, and context. For any given person, then, it is always the context of interaction that determines the level of speech opted for.

An analogous decision must be made when using what in English are called personal pronouns. "Japanese has historically used an enormous variety of words to refer to speaker, persons spoken to, and persons spoken of. . . . Japanese has this enormous lexicon of 'personal pronouns' because it never really had any 'personal pronouns' at all" (Miller 1967: 341). What I will call Japanese personal referents are in point of fact nouns that indicate categories and degrees of communicative distance. The selection of one from among the great array of such referents will reflect the human and social relationships that obtain between the two parties. There are no fixed points, either "self" or "other," and as I have already remarked, it is of the utmost significance that designation of the other invariably precedes designation of the self in any interaction.

Another quite remarkable feature of personal referents in Japan is the great rapidity with which they have changed historically. Most of those found in Meiji letters and diaries of only a century ago, no less than almost the entire inventory of personal referents widely employed in the Tokugawa period, have passed out of use almost completely.[3] The great majority of them are words that originally denoted place or direction, or were titles, all successively diverted to suggestive or euphemistic usages intended to imply degree of distance of relationship between speaker and hearer. The developmental career of these terms is well attested. Originally connoting the expression of deference by the speaker, they gradually shift to express the speaker's superiority, then are used only to inferiors, and finally are dropped altogether except for the few that survive in deliberate insults (Suzuki 1978: 98–99). There is little need to resort to profanity in a language where the use of an inappropriately high or low referential term is quite enough to inflict a grievous insult.

During the upheavals on Japanese university campuses in the 1960s, this was a tactic employed brilliantly by the students. In meetings with members of the faculty, the students bent every effort to demolish the linguistic markers of relative status by using styles of address and reference of the most demeaning sort. The more senior the faculty member, the more devastating the effect of this deliberate leveling or inverting of status indicators. Toward the end of a roundtable discussion held in 1968 between striking students and a group of professors of Tokyo University, the novelist Mishima Yukio, who as an alumnus had been invited to participate, burst out impatiently and demanded of one of the faculty: "Why don't you speak on equal terms with them? If they use insulting terms, you should reply in kind!" There was no answer; the professor could neither tolerate the humiliation nor summon the wrath required to destroy the habit of a lifetime.

The Western reader must wonder if the matter of personal referents can really be so complicated. The answer must be an unequivocal "yes."[4] By the age of three, children in the United States have generally mastered the distinction between "I" and "you," two personal pronouns that will serve them throughout life in all interactions with others. Furthermore, in the daily speech of the American child, these two terms are heavily favored over all other possible personal referents, such as name, kin term, and the like. The Japanese male child, for his part, by the age of six must master the use of at least six terms of self-reference; girls of that age will employ five. (For persons addressed or referred to, the situation is even more complicated, for both boys and girls regularly use a minimum of fourteen such terms.) Japanese children also use names, kin terms, and place names, but the really striking contrast with the American child's speech habits is that none of the possible options is clearly dominant among Japanese children. With overwhelming frequency they use no self-referent of any kind.

What is more, the acquisition of personal referents does not end in childhood in Japan, but instead continues throughout adult life at least into middle age. As individuals mature, they are required to deal with an ever more complex social world within which they may maintain some but must alter many of the ways in which they refer to themselves and others. The calculus is first learned in the family, of course, where children quickly discover that they may not use personal referents in addressing or directly referring to any person senior to them, whereas to their juniors they may employ such forms freely. It is a skill, this ability to sort out people in terms of status, sex, and age, that is mastered early. Not surprisingly, the use of personal referents is one of the most difficult features of the language to teach Americans, for whom the apparently irreducible "I" presents a major stumbling block to the easy adoption of the constantly shifting, relational "I" of the Japanese, which is not detached from the other, "and thus stays immersed in the world" (Miyoshi 1979: 123).

Even the reading (pronunciation) of the characters with which one's name is written may vary contextually, so that an individual is called by one reading[5] of his name by one set of associates and by another among members of another group.

One such person was the noted ethnologist Ariga (Aruga) Kizaemon. Several years ago, an American colleague of mine was compiling a bibliography of Japanese social science works on a particular topic. As it was to be used primarily by foreign scholars, the names of authors were to be given in roman letters and in characters as well. I remarked in passing as I looked over the alphabetized list that he had decided to romanize this man's name Ariga rather than Aruga. He immediately demanded to know which was correct, and refused to accept my (as he saw it) indefensibly ambiguous answer that either would do. In order to settle the matter to his satisfaction, I wrote to an associate of the famous man, who was then still alive, and asked him which was correct. I received the following illuminating reply:

I am fortunate to be able to send you this latest answer from the professor himself. Of course we know that he is called Aruga in his local community of Suwa, Nagano Prefecture, and by his older intimate friends from his earliest days in Tokyo. But at a later time, both in Japanese society and internationally, he became more commonly known as Ariga. Nevertheless, when I wrote his brief biography in Japanese in 1958, I put the phonetic reading *a-ru-ga* beside the two characters with which the name is written. Now I think that I must change my opinion, for this is what he told me. In 1938, when he published a book in Japanese whose title was to appear in French in the colophon, he decided on the romanization after debating whether Aruga or Arouga would yield a more accurate pronunciation by speakers of French. He decided on Arouga. Later he looked into other surnames with the same first character and found that all were read *ari* rather than *aru*. Now everyone named Aruga comes from or is descended from people whose native place is Suwa, but some who have migrated to other parts of the country have changed the pronunciation to Ariga. He therefore concluded that Aruga is a localism, and that he should switch to the more standard Ariga. This explains why although the first printing of his 1943 book *Nihon kazoku/seido/to kosaku seido* carries the phonetic syllables a-ru-ga beside the characters, he requested that the publisher delete them in the second printing, letting the characters stand alone to be pronounced as the reader saw fit. Naturally, most people will therefore read the name Ariga. What is the situation today? A few persons around him call him Aruga. Some people, like myself, sometimes called him Ariga, at other times Aruga; most people call him Ariga. When he publishes in English, the professor himself uses the form Ariga, so this is probably the one your colleague should use in his bibliography.[6]

In short, in the view of both men, there was no "correct" reading of the name, and in this we may be tempted to find yet more evidence for that contingency of self to which I have referred.

There is another complication. The large number of referents and the manner in which they are employed indicates that even the question "Who is self; who is other?" is not unambiguously settled from the onset of interaction. There are, for example, terms that can be used for self-reference as well as second-person and third-person reference. That is, some common terms such as *boku* or *temae* may mean "I" or "you"—they are interchangeable lexical items in the spoken language. In English usage, by contrast, the speaker stands at the center of the set of referents he or she will employ. Does this circumstance imply, then, that in Japan all interpersonal interaction takes place in a blur of ambiguity and confusion? Actually, it is sometimes so, but a safer conclusion is that the identification of self and other is always indeterminate in the sense that there is no fixed center from which, in effect, the individual asserts a noncontingent existence.[7]

These two features of the language—*keigo* and personal referents—permeate all daily interaction. Some years ago, I invited a Japanese friend, in town for a brief visit, to come to my home to meet several of the Japanese who teach at my university. They had already gathered when he arrived, and as

I took his coat before showing him into the room where they
were waiting, he asked the one question whose answer would
facilitate the initial interaction with this group of total strangers: How old are they? Armed with the information that most
of them were slightly older that he, he was secure in his adoption of the proper speech level. They in turn took their cue
from his opening presentation of himself, based squarely on
his prior definition of their status on that basic dimension of
chronological age.

When strangers meet in Japan, an almost invariant form of
behavior among men is the exchange of cards. Although they
also serve the practical purpose of indicating the characters
with which the personal name is written, which as we will
see is a matter of considerable complexity, their primary purpose is to reveal at once the social status of each party through
the titles or affiliations printed on them. The recipient of a
card has been given an invaluable clue to the level of speech
it is appropriate for him to adopt. I think this is not an over-
reading on my part, for many men have two different cards,
the public one that carries name, rank in his organization, and
business address and telephone number, and another that bears
only his name, home address, and home telephone number.
The latter is a personal card, given out only to those who are
to be admitted to the closed circle of one's acquaintances.

It is when some awful miscalculation of relative position
has been made that one can see in the nature of the corrective
action taken the degree of importance assigned proper levels
of speech. I am indebted to an American colleague, who was
at the time an advanced graduate student, for an illuminating
example of such behavior. He had gone to the office of one of
Japan's leading professors of sociology shortly after arriving in
Japan for the first time. There he introduced himself, and they
chatted for a few minutes before he produced a letter of introduction from his American faculty adviser. The professor read

it, rose abruptly, and left the office without a word. A few minutes later a young man entered, introduced himself as a graduate student in sociology, and offered to show the visiting American around. As they were leaving, the professor came back, and without speaking to either of them, returned to his desk. It was only much later, when his spoken Japanese had improved considerably, that my informant realized that the combination of his own initial adoption of a presumptuous level of speech and the inability of most Japanese to assess the chronological age of Caucasians—who, it should be noted, not only all look alike but invariably look older than they are—had misled the distinguished gentleman into using a far too deferential speech pattern toward a stranger whom he had mistakenly assumed to be a colleague.

Many Japanese, especially younger people, are impatient with this line of argument. They will assure you that there has been a marked tendency to reduce these complexities in the postwar period.[8] To some extent they are right, for in straightforward encounters of a mundane sort, fewer levels of politeness are now in use than was the case only a generation ago. Nevertheless, even in a group of people that claims total unconcern with status distinctions, it is usually quite easy for an observer to sort out the implicit hierarchy among them by careful assessment of the way in which personal referents and status language are used by its members in speaking to one another. The language has not yet appreciably enriched its status-neutral vocabulary.

Let us now turn to other ways in which people present themselves in social contexts. It will be recalled that Japanese children generally employ no self-referents at all in ordinary speech. It is also the case that a person is generally expected to call as little attention to himself as possible. The word most commonly used in this connection is *enryo*, "restraint" or "reserve." One way to express *enryo* is to avoid giving opinions and to sidestep choices when they are offered. As a matter of fact, choices are less often offered in Japan than in the United States. In this connection, the psychiatrist Doi Takeo (1973: 12) has given us a charming account of one kind of excessive strain he experienced during his first visit to the United States:

Another thing that made me nervous was the custom whereby an American host will ask a guest, before a meal, whether he would prefer a strong or a soft drink. Then, if the guest asks for liquor, he will ask him whether, for example, he prefers scotch or bourbon. When the guest has made this decision, he next has to give instructions as to how much he wishes to drink, and how he wants it served. With the main meal, fortunately, one has only to eat what one is served, but once it is over one has to choose whether to take coffee or tea, and—in even greater detail—whether one wants it with sugar, milk, and so on. . . . I could not have cared less.

The strain must have been considerable, for in Japan, by contrast, the host, having carefully considered what is most likely to please this particular guest, will simply place before him a succession of an overwhelming number of items of food and drink, all of which he is urged to consume, in the standard phrase, "without *enryo.*" It is incumbent on the guest to eat and drink at least part of everything offered him, whether or not he likes the particular item, in order not to give offense by appearing to rebuke his host for miscalculating what would please him.

Another feature of interaction is the great importance assigned to place, in the physical sense of relative location. As we have seen, many personal referents were originally designations of place. The relative placing of members of a group in the context of interaction is still a matter of great moment. In a Japanese room, the seat of honor is that furthest from the entrance, and the pileup of people in a doorway, all unwilling to take a seat first, is likely to be the result of a combination of genuine confusion and the expression of seemly *enryo.* In no context is precedence accorded some absolute position, and Japanese culture lacks entirely the cross-culturally familiar priority assigned to right over left, or indeed much concern with the distinction.[9] Like relational personal referents, that too is a calculus that often defeats and usually irritates the foreigner. In 1853 the Russian Goncharov, in Japan to negotiate with domain officials, seems to have been permanently infuriated by the concern for ceremony and the placement of the parties to the negotiations. In his journal, we find the following despairing comment:

In Europe, people are worrying at this moment about whether to be or not to be, but we argued for whole days about whether to sit or not to sit, to stand or not to stand, and [those issues resolved] how we should sit and what we should sit on. . . .[10]

To his credit, Goncharov did realize early on that for the Japanese negotiators, on the resolution of these matters turned the all-important definition of the relative bargaining strengths of the two parties.

In Japan today there remains more emphasis on ceremony and ritual than the casual American driver of a Honda automobile or owner of a Seiko watch could possibly imagine. They serve primarily to mark the initiation and termination of interaction, and above all to locate persons and actions clearly in time and space. In this connection, the comment of a Korean woman living in Japan is instructive. Her view of Japanese society and the Japanese is otherwise rather hostile, but she says approvingly: "People [here] give a lot of time and effort to rituals and ceremonies. . . . Human life, after all, is a very chaotic thing. And the Japanese . . . are able to create at least the semblance of order" (Bell 1973: 145–6).

Not only spatial position, but time schedules as well, are relative and contingent. An alert American soon learns to make the entries in an appointment book in pencil, for almost everyone is prepared to suggest mutual adjustments, post-

ponements, and compromises. As all are flexible in these matters, none suffers particularly from the virtually universal operation of what I have modestly come to call Smith's Law of
Flexible Time, which may be put simply: "The most recently
contracted engagement takes precedence over all those contracted earlier." It is sufficient to offer only the explanation
(really a nonexplanation) that otherwise unspecified circumstances have made it inconvenient to honor the original commitment. An American I know who was back in Japan after
a lengthy absence made a revealing comment about the effect
of this practice on him: "I had forgotten that your time is not
your own here!" It is an accurate observation; everyone's time
is everyone's.

And so we come at last to the crucial question. Where in
this semblance of order of a highly relational kind does individuality lie? Miyoshi (1974: 78–79), ever the Cassandra, believes
that the Japanese are left without a personality: "The young
Japanese studies his assigned role until he perfects it. His
worth will be measured by his approximation to the ideal of
his type. . . ." The judgment is no doubt too severe, but in
fact one hears on every hand characterizations of persons by
the extent to which they do approximate an ideal role type.
The word is *rashisa* (in its adjectival form *rashi*), and it is
ordinarily attached to the name of a role or status. Thus,
gakusei-rashi, okusan-rashi, gunjin-rashi—"the very model of"
a student, wife, soldier, respectively. A person who fails to
conform to the idealized role or status is said to be "not at all
like" (*rashikunai*) that ideal. More pejoratively, it may be
said of a person that he or she has too strong a personality
(*kosei ga tsuyoi*). A young man, for instance, may be warned
that the girl he wishes to marry is simply not material for
becoming sufficiently wifelike because her personality is too
salient. Broadcast descriptions of suspected perpetrators of
crimes customarily note that eyewitnesses describe the person

as studentlike, officeworkerlike, or gangsterlike, reflecting their assessment of demeanor, clothing, and other clues to social identity. Since the individual who is perceived of as the very model of the role or status he or she occupies is ordinarily accorded some respect for this achievement, it is frequently taken by foreign and Japanese observers alike that the ultimate goal of the individual is the complete suppression of the self or, more drastically, that the Japanese have no sense of the self at all. The conclusion does not follow.

Let us begin with the matter of personal, "given" names. Despite what I have said above about the importance of context in determining so basic a matter as the pronunciation of a person's surname, there is less ambiguity in the realm of family names than obtains with respect to the reading of the character or characters with which the personal, given name is written. Many years ago when I was using the University of Michigan's collection of Japanese-language books, I noticed that the cards for those written by an internationally known scholar had all been changed. The typed form of his given name had been crossed out and another reading penciled in above it. This good man had used the collection himself, and finding that the cataloguers had mistakenly romanized his name according to the reading given that character in the dictionaries, had quietly crossed it out and written in the reading that he used. It is just such near chaos that led a librarian to remark to me once that she would like to have a grant to go to Japan simply to ask as many scholars as she could arrange to meet how their names were to be romanized. For those who were deceased, she expected that the information could be got from family members or close friends.

Sometimes the character for a given name is read idiosyncratically, but often what appears to be such a reading may in fact represent a family tradition. It used to be the custom in some families of rank or attainment to give its sons names of which the first character was identical. Thus, four brothers might be named Hide plus another character—Hidezō, Hidetoshi, Hideo, and Hidematsu. Not uncommonly, the reading of that shared character was unique to the family, and there was no way to discover the "real" pronunciation other than to ask. But then the Japanese do not much use given names, either in conversation with the individual or in referring to him, limiting such familiarity to members of the family and one's most intimate circle of friends. (It is for this reason that in the immediate postwar years many Japanese adopted foreign given names by which their American acquaintances or employers could address them. There were, in those days, many Bettys, Lindas, Bills, and Bobs.) It is apparent, then, that the personal name is closely tied to the notion of the person. It may be uniquely that person's, but even if it is one of the most common in the population, others will not use it lightly.

Indeed, so closely related are name and individual that many parents give great care to the selection of names for their children. There are auspicious names, cautionary ones, and names of great beauty. The last are not those that have a pleasing sound necessarily; their beauty lies in the characters with which they are written. The notion that the name is closely linked to the fate of the individual is reflected in the existence of a profession in Japan, that of name selection (*seimei-handan*). Its practitioners are sought out by people who wish to change their luck by changing their given names, and it is a thriving business.

In death as in life, individual and name are inseparable, for on the back of the memorial tablet placed in the ancestral altar, whose face bears the posthumous name bestowed on the deceased by the priest, is the name-in-life of the person memorialized. The dead are not, as is so often alleged, an anonymous aggregate of the spirits of the ancestors, at least in the years immediately following death.[11] Now all of this may be dismissed as an oddity of no great import, but I would suggest that an attitude of fundamental importance is being expressed in the simple fact that a great many personal names and a not inconsiderable proportion of family names in Japan can be rendered with assurance only by the individual, his or her kin, and intimate friends.

It seems to me that the Japanese possess a very clear sense of self, although it differs from our own, and that they regularly behave as though persons are indeed individuals. Western observers are often blinded by our inability to perceive the locus of the self in Japan, and by our unwillingness to accept the low priority given its expression. "The American achetype . . . seems more attuned to cultivating a self that knows it is unique in the cosmos, the Japanese archetype to a self that can feel human in the company of others" (Plath 1980: 218). There is a widespread and quite mistaken belief that in Japan the individual who occupies an ascriptive status in the family household of his birth simply grows up to occupy pseudo-ascriptive statuses in pseudo-household groupings in the wider society. Such is far from the case.

It is a commonplace to remark that the members of a Japanese household are identified primarily by their relative positions in it, but as I have tried to show, there are good reasons why even these positions are not ranked on a fixed scale of absolute hierarchy. It is less routinely pointed out that recruitment into the permanent positions in a household is with great frequency made on completely nonascriptive grounds. Persons recruited into the position of successor-head and his wife always enter them as adults, and neither need have been born into the house in question. The frequent adoption of successors shows clearly that the Japanese household is essentially an enterprise group, not a descent organization, and that passing over a son in favor of an adopted successor for the headship among merchants, craftsmen, and artists is a

manifestation of a universalistic element in the definition of
the role of the household head. Although a man would prefer
that the succession pass to his eldest son or, failing that,
through a daughter for whom he adopts a husband, the overriding considerations determining the choice of successor are
the highly pragmatic ones of competence and availability
(Befu 1962: 40).

The widespread practice of a bewildering variety of forms
of adoption involves yet another principle. People do not
generally unite to form groups, not even households, but are
instead recruited into them. One's sense of self is enhanced
by being selected to join a group, and the standing of that
group is in turn enhanced by its ability to attract individuals
of quality and achievement. Once taken in, however, powerful
sanctions—of which the threat of ostracism is only the most
severe—are brought to bear on the individual, who is expected
to pursue personal interests only to the extent that the other
members of the group agree that such a course does not contravene principles of harmony and effective performance. The
individual cannot act out of self-interest that violates the consensus of the group. The usual alternatives are to suppress
personal desires, to modify one's preferences in acceptable
ways, or to leave the group altogether. Yet the general preference for consensual decisions does leave the system extremely
vulnerable to those who seek to impose their will on the majority. The insistent dissenters often get their way simply because
others will not employ like tactics to oppose them.

But leaving the group, the choice among the three that
most Americans would probably favor, is a step not easily
taken in Japan, for the simple reason of the clear boundaries
that surround the group and set it off from all the others. The
members of one social group try not to concern themselves
with the business of other groups, "letting them pursue their
interests and avoiding [any action] which may provoke the

intervention of 'outsiders' " (Kogane 1975: 191–2). Lateral movement from one group to another is thus very difficult, for it is a matter not of being accepted, but of being invited into a new one. Because the society offers few options and extremely restricted choices for individual mobility, some are moved to emigrate and thus escape it completely. Escape seems to many the only recourse, for "The misfortune of the Japanese is that they have been unable [to accept] the concept of legitimate opposition between self and other" (Morisaki 1973: 161–2).

At this point I will have lost those of my readers who vigorously decry the tendency to represent Japan as a country of consensus and harmony, where the qualities of hierarchy and authority, loyalty and obedience dominate the lives of an essentially faceless population.[12] As I admitted in the Introduction, there is a considerable risk involved in the attempt to present a normative picture of this very complex society, although it is by now apparent that I think it both possible and profitable to do so. Is there no diversity and variability, then? As a matter of fact, both are readily observable in Japanese society and behavior, and to ignore them is to misrepresent a significant characteristic of life in that country.

I do not mean the kind of variations that any good social scientist is concerned with, such as the differences in the lives of those at the very top and the very bottom of the economic scale, men and women, blue-collar and white-collar workers, and the like. Neither am I particularly concerned to expose the dark side of life that contrasts so sharply with the bright face of the newly affluent Japan. That dark side exists, of course, but within it we should discover many of the same principles that I have so far dealt with in full operation. I have made almost no reference to Japan's minority populations—the Koreans and Chinese, the offspring of mixed parentage, the remnants of the Ainu of the northern island of Hokkaido, or the largest of them all, the untouchables (*buraku-min*), who are estimated to number between 1 and 3 million.[13] Nor do the differences in personality that one encounters on every hand seem to me to be especially worthy of attention in this context. To be sure there are bullies, very rude people, panderers, flatterers, the downright dishonest and unpleasant, hopeless misfits, murderers, suicides, the mentally ill, and the psychologically crippled. No serious student of Japan has ever suggested that the Japanese are all alike or that Japanese behavior is so stereotyped that it can be said of individuals what a teacher of mine used to say of the great Buddhist temples of Nara and Kyoto: "If you've seen one, you've seen them all!"

These disadvantaged populations and their condition have been dealt with more or less satisfactorily by others. What I find more arresting about the existence of diversity and variability in Japanese society is that its own members so regularly are moved to remark instead that it is just the opposite—highly invariable (R. J. Smith 1977). We have already had the acerbic testimony of Miyoshi to the effect that the Japanese novelist lacks access to the materials essential to his craft—varied life experiences and the presence of vivid personalities in his surroundings.[14] He is by no means alone in that harsh judgment, which I have heard put in many different ways by Japanese friends and acquaintances. Yet to an even greater degree than we outsiders, the Japanese are perfectly well aware that it is not so. Rather than dismiss the claim of uniformity, we are compelled to treat the observation itself as a datum.

Why do the Japanese routinely express the opinion that theirs is so unusually uniform a society? Perhaps they are saying only that in the long run such differences as do exist are of negligible importance. Or it may be they perceive that it is only in limited areas of life where variant behavior is negatively sanctioned, leaving the rest fluid and supple, open to divergent interpretations and action on the part of the individual. That is, it may well be the general attitude that so long as a limited number of public things are done in a socially approved way, there simply is no reason to take note of variation in the realm of private behavior, much less condemn it. If we assume that people are well aware of the variability, then we shall have to concede a peculiar strength to their view that seems to assess differences as though they were similarities, or of no moment.

But there is another side to the coin. What is one observer's invariability may seem to another very like great diversity. Within the confines of Japanese society, there are indeed some spheres of activity of which the common view is that there is diversity aplenty. The difficulty is that the differences which are pointed out in support of this contention are often so minute that they are scarcely discernible to the eye of the foreigner. For example, it is routinely noted that one of the major tasks confronting the new bride is learning "the ways of the house" (*kafū*) of her husband. In the past, her failure to do so often served as the rationale for sending her back to her natal house. On the face of it, this is an extraordinary claim. What are the ways of the house? Does the inner working of every household in Japan really differ so drastically from that of all the rest that a new recruit can possibly find it so difficult to master it? It seems unlikely, but however that may be, we must at least ask why it is so important for members of a household to maintain that theirs is in significant ways different from all others.

An even more striking example comes from the world of the arts and crafts. The adherents of each school of a particular art will assert with almost fanatical insistence that theirs is different in important particulars from all its rivals. Each school of dance, flower arranging, tea ceremony, calligraphy, martial arts, and all others that require training has its secrets, which at the proper time will be imparted to the disciple or pupil by the head of the school. As one advances in the ranks or grades of proficiency, the teacher reveals additional secrets of the art, enabling the aficionado to detect by the most subtle of signs that the performer has risen to a certain level of skill. Save for those who have devoted themselves to the study of one or another of these arts and crafts, no observer, least of all the uninitiated foreigner, can appreciate the distinctions thus signaled. In this connection, it is important to note that at least one advantage to the claim of uniqueness in practice and performance in this context is financial, for the founders and teachers of schools sell certificates of proficiency to their pupils, and license them to teach in turn.

The assertion that the ways of the house and the teachings of the school are in some senses unique is very closely related to the importance of these groups for their membership. The distinction between inside (*uchi*) and outside (*soto*) is a fundamental one in contemporary Japan (Lebra 1976: 112–13). It should therefore come as no surprise that there is a corresponding emphasis on the distinctiveness of each group. It is within these closed spheres of Japanese society that we find the clearest evidence for exclusivity—what "we" of our group know and do is unlike what "they" of their group believe and practice. It is for the newly recruited members of any group to master the details of its unique heritage.

Even the person who will tell you that conformity is the rule in the society nonetheless participates to some extent in activities that are not standardized by societal rules. Such variability occurs in what is for most Japanese the one religious activity in which they are most likely to engage, the conduct of memorial rites for the ancestors of the household.

In some households and in some communities, any given altar may contain the tablets of senior ascendants and a great variety of other ancestors. In the house next door or in some houses in the next community down the road, tablets may be limited to agnatic kin. In some regions only one child (the successor) is accorded the right and duty of caring for the ancestors, and none of the other children makes copies of the tablets for his own domestic altar; in some places all sons may receive a copy of a parent's tablet; and in still others a copy is given to all children, sons and daughters alike. In still other places all altars in effect hold bilateral tablets of the kin of both husband and wife. In a single village one finds that the souls of children of the household are held by some to require special treatment of a kind elsewhere given only to the dangerous wandering ghosts of strangers, while the neighbors reject out of hand the notion that the spirits of one's own dead child could be potentially harmful. All households in the community I am referring to are longtime residents of the village, and do not differ markedly in occupation, economic status, or ethnic origin. In most rural communities, people say that the ancestral spirits are passively benign or altogether powerless, but we have accounts of some places where they are regularly charged with causing misfortune. For most Japanese households the aim of the ancestral rites is to comfort the spirits, to express gratitude to them for past favors, and to ask them to protect the family. (R. J. Smith 1974: 344)

But at least one of the New Religions teaches that the faithful must sever all karmic links with their ancestors in order to avoid an evil fate, whereas another urges its converts to collect as many memorial tablets as possible and to offer prayers on behalf of the spirits they represent.

Perhaps the variant possibilities I have mentioned above are best viewed as merely superficial in the sense that they diverge from a common theme or core. Simply stated, that core belief might be said to be that the living are linked to the dead in such a way that either can affect the fate of the other. But surely we have lost a very great deal by moving to such a level of generality. Can it be of so little importance that for some people and for members of some religious groups

today the spirits of the dead are malign, whereas for others
they are either benign or passively dependent on the ministra-
tions of the living? It is, of course, a distinction of great importance, but there have been few attempts to analyze even
these fundamental differences, for they seem not to covary
with other phenomena in predictable ways. It is not that no
sense can be made of them; it is rather that we have done very
little to pursue the meaning of diversity for the Japanese.

I do not wish to leave the impression that conformity is
always of so public a nature, and that nonconformity is always
so private and by some standards of such a pale and shadowy
character. Nonconformists do exist, of course, and Ivan Morris
(1975: xxi) has directed our attention to a kind of hero
particularly revered in Japan: ". . . the man whose single-
minded sincerity will not allow him to make the manoeuvers
and compromises that are so often needed for success." These
heroes exemplify the nobility of failure, their lives and careers
ending in utter defeat for both the man and his cause. Morris
(1975: 228) concludes that "a strong non-conformist nature
[is] especially admired in Japan because so rare." So, by implication, is sincerity as it is normally understood in the West.
The word is the usual translation of the Japanese *makoto*,
which has a rather broad range of meanings—"single-hearted,"
"devoted," "honest," and "loyal" among them. About men
of sincerity there is an unmistakable quality of single-minded-
ness (Frager and Rohlen 1976:257–8) that often lends to
their course of action a kind of stunning simplicity and purity.

On November 25, 1970, Mishima Yukio, one of Japan's
leading novelists and playwrights, dressed in the uniform of
his small paramilitary group, the Shield Society, went with
four aides to the Tokyo headquarters of the Japan Self-Defense
Forces. After seizing the office and the person of the director,
Mishima appeared on the balcony outside. There he harangued
a growing crowd of soldiers, appealing to them to act to restore

imperial rule and lead the people to reject the gross consumer-ism that in his view had come close to destroying the true Japanese spirit. Jeered and booed by his audience, he retired into the director's office where he committed *seppuku,* the more elegant term for *hara-kiri.*[15] The warrior's ultimate ges-ture of sincerity, ritual suicide was often used in the past both as the severest form of censure of a wayward or unresponsive target, and a final effort to enlist the sympathies and energies of those who might be prepared to rally to the cause and carry on the work of the dead hero. More often than not, however, *seppuku* was the final act of a doomed leader.

In another age Mishima might well have become a classic hero, for his failure was undeniably complete. Yet even though his last desperate attempt to persuade his countrymen to re-turn to the path of virtue as he interpreted it was dismissed by the prime minister as the act of a madman, and to most Japanese proved more puzzling than galvanizing, it cannot be denied that he struck a responsive chord. Shortly after the event, I found myself in the company of a sixteen-year-old high school student. In appearance the boy personified the alien-ated youth of Japan of the early 1970s—straight hair long enough to brush his shoulders, dark glasses, blue jeans and T-shirt, and an American flag ("I would *never* wear a Japanese flag," he had told me indignantly when I raised the obvious question) sewn on the back of his leather jacket. Sensing that our worlds overlapped somewhat less than perfectly, I was at a loss to think of a profitable topic of conversation when the cover of a magazine on a nearby newsstand caught my eye.

"What," I asked, "do you think of Mishima's death?"

He replied, "It is the only sincere political act that has taken place in Japan since the end of the war."

"Does that mean that you believe in what he stood for?"

"Of course not!" The boy looked genuinely appalled at the suggestion. "But I admire his sincerity."

In the years I have known him since that conversation I have never heard this young man pay that ultimate compliment to any other person. Perhaps it is because men of a nonconformist nature are so rare, as Morris maintained, that acts of sincerity draw approbation even from those to whom the principles involved are anathema.[16]

Conformity thus appears to be a virtue, while certain kinds of extreme nonconformity are regarded as more virtuous still. Can that mean that the less than heroic Japanese never fret or complain about their lot or chafe at the strictures imposed upon them by their society? Are they wholly acquiescent in succumbing to the pressures that would eradicate their personalities and lead them totally to suppress any temptation to express what remains of their sense of self? Worse yet, might it be that they never even come to realize that they have an autonomous existence? Not at all, and one need look no further than the popular literature and drama of the country for evidence to contravene any such easy assumptions as those just set out. A recurrent theme in novels, plays, and film is the exploration of the ways in which the young and strong-willed attempt to resolve the conflicts that arise in the process of coming to terms with the demands of society. Those who fail to do so, whether because they will not or cannot, are the tragic heroes and heroines of fiction and the press, for whom the only solution is suicide. For ordinary mortals, however, there are in daily use many words that reflect recognition of the need to accommodate, to endure, to bear, to accept, and to relinquish—*gaman, shimbo, akirame* among them. All are words in daily use to children, kin, friends, and colleagues whom one is urging to come to terms—and thereby demonstrate neither submissiveness nor passivity, but true maturity.[17]

The society provides a number of ways in which the individual can acquire the recommended fortitude. At all levels of Japanese society, one finds a marked interest in the development of what is called *seishin*, "spirit."[18] The concept of the "Japanese spirit" (*Yamato damashi*) was much used during the Greater East Asia War by propagandists who asserted that it would surely be victorious over gross Western materialism. They were so utterly wrong that this specifically jingoistic embodiment of *seishin* doctrine today appeals only to tiny but clamorous groups on the far political right. In its contemporary form, then, *seishin* training is thought to lead to the attainment of purely practical rather than transcendental ends, such as better performance in school or at work or a happier family life. The stricter and more arduous the training, the more it is thought to serve the aim of constantly polishing one's character. Through discipline and adversity a person achieves self-development and, crucially, self-mastery.

The study of calligraphy, flower arranging, tea ceremony, dance, musical instruments, and of course the martial arts are but a few of the undertakings to which principles of *seishin* training apply. There are innumerable schools of all of these, each headed by a teacher or master. The authority of the head of the school is absolute, far more so than that exercised by the heads of "real" households. It is believed that the more demanding the teacher, the more valuable the training, and it is at the head of some of these groups that Japan's true autocrats are to be found. Their style is also found in the world of modern sports, as anyone will know who has viewed the fifth episode of a television series called "Olympiad," prepared for the 1976 games. The program, which concerns the exploits of women in the Olympics from the 1912 games through those of 1968, includes a segment on a training session of the Japanese women's volleyball team, whose coach inevitably is a male.[19] The regimen shown is brutal, and following a particularly grueling practice session the team members are ordered to line up. The coach walks down the file, pausing occasionally to administer a tongue-lashing and a sharp slap to the face of a player. When I expressed my reservations to some Japanese friends about the scene, one of them said: "That's a very American reaction. Do teams with easygoing coaches win Olympic gold medals?" I cannot answer that question, but this one had done so in 1964, defeating the formidable Russian women's team in the Tokyo games.

It is not the case that all teachers of the arts and sports and crafts employ such harsh disciplinary tactics, although some do. What makes such treatment tolerable is one thing alone; the pupil must remain firmly convinced of the absolute justice and impartiality of the teacher's assessment of his or her progress. Through intense application, strict obedience, and long apprenticeship, the pupil may one day hope to approach the level of competence that will wring a word of praise from the teacher. And as with the success of communication, there is a strong tendency to attribute failure to the recipient of the training rather than to any inadequacy on the part of the teacher.

The person who has mastered a skill that requires the perfection of *seishin* is believed to have acquired as well a general competence and self-discipline that will enable him or her to undertake new and quite unrelated tasks. In the pursuit of the goals of *seishin*, therefore, one seeks out a stern teacher who is devoted to the art, craft or skill, and submits unconditionally to his or her authority. The good character thus developed "makes one a good follower, loyal and unquestioning (and also, at the appropriate time, a good leader)" (Frager and Rohlen 1976:260–1). The prevailing view is that life is an unending path of accomplishment, and that character development is a long-term process that can only be enhanced by delaying rewards and making the ambitious wait. Unlike the heroes of Horatio Alger's stories, who seem to be born honest and true and strong, those of the typical Japanese success story become all these things through suffering, perseverance, and obedience. The injunction that guides the pupil is *messhi hōkō*, "destroy ego and serve others." But there is more to it even than this, for a person's character, a person's spirit, is revealed ultimately in that person's accomplishments (1976: 258). One of the motivations in seeking a piece of calligraphy by a noted person, if I may be forgiven the pun, is that it objectively embodies evidence of that individual's strength of character. The person and the work are one.

I have no intention here of propping up the sad American misconception about the place of Zen Buddhism in Japanese culture. Zen austerities represent the essence of this style of training, but it must be remembered that in Japan *seishin* training is found in a great variety of activities and institutions. At the more affluent levels of the society, we do find heavy emphasis on formal Zen techniques, including harsh discipline and the concept of the unity of art and spirit. Among institutions that attract the less advantaged, such as the New Religions, however, the training is less rigorous and the emphasis on the intensely practical, in the sense that it is maintained that the person who develops *seishin* will enjoy good health, overcome obstacles to success, and achieve economic well-being. There is also a large element of *seishin* philosophy, bordering on the touchingly naive, in the programs of a very large number of volunteer organizations, which tend to set their sights much lower, aiming "at creating a simple, bright spirit of kindness and good-will among men" (1976: 261). In all the transformations of the basic philosophy, the central concern is with the development of a positive inner attitude, by means of which external constraints can be overcome and difficulties resolved. In the last analysis, however, *seishin* philosophy also teaches one to come to terms with the world as it is, and to remember that one's ambitions may well prove to exceed one's abilities.

Yet it is not solely through coming to terms with the demands of society that the individual can find self-realization. There are other ways of achieving that end that will be readily understandable even to those whose own sense of self stops with the skin. For the Japanese, individuality lies at the opposite pole from social involvement. The autonomy of the individual is protected and assured not in society, but away from it, where one may legitimately indulge in self-reflection and introspection. It is the latter route that leads into one's true heart (*kokoro*) and puts one once again in contact with one's true nature—one's *hara* ("belly") and self (*jibun*). It is in these inner realms that truth and integrity are thought to lie (Lebra 1976: 158–61).

It is surely the case, however, that the number of people who seek simple relief from frustration is far greater than the number of those who seek complete autonomy. In Japan, I would suggest, such relief is obtained through seeking the fusion of the self and the objective world in which that self lives (Lebra 1976: 163). It is this imperative that informs all Japanese systems of psychological therapy whose chief aim is to reintegrate individuals into the family and their small part of the objective social world. It is also a chief promise of the New Religions that through faith their followers will come to understand the virtue of assuming their proper place according to their abilities and capacities, when finally they come to realize their own limitations.

I have recently come across some excellent examples of this teaching in action in *Dharma World*, the English-language publication of the lay Buddhist organization called Risshō kōsei kai. Every issue of the magazine carries one of a series of confessional articles by members of the group, with titles such as "How I Opened My Eyes to True Love," "Transcending Vengeance," "Awaking to My True Nature," and "Start by Changing Yourself." Each writer gives an account of his or her history of antisocial acts and feelings, and details the suffering they caused others and themselves by their failure to maintain harmonious relations within their families or with their workmates. All then tell how a member of the Risshō kōsei kai opened their eyes to the teachings of the Buddha, thereby enabling them to restore their homes, their careers, and their peace of mind. They end by having come to terms with themselves and the objective demands of society.

In the Japanese reading of Confucianism, the centerpiece of the cosmos is human society and its manifold human relationships. Shinto likewise suggests that since the world is absolute, it must be confronted realistically (Reischauer 1977: 139; Bell 1973: 9). Having accomplished fusion with the objective world, however, the person is urged to cultivate his or her individual nature, which by definition is to be accomplished in socially approved ways. To an extent not even remotely approached in the United States, most Japanese have "their own personal literary, artistic, or performing skill [which] is not only a means of emotional self-expression, but a treasured element of self-identity" (Reischauer 1977: 149). For the Japanese, the acquisition of a skill is essentially an act of individual will, and the mastery of a skill is viewed as the outcome of the development of the inner self (1977: 152). This is so much the case that I have often been surprised by the revelation of quite unreasonable ambitions and expectation of attainment on the part of my Japanese friends and acquaintances, who appear to feel they can achieve any goal through the application of sheer effort. But by and large what is most admired is control. Only the person who has the inner strength to discipline himself or herself, to conform if you prefer, is accorded the respect thought due a truly mature person. The Japanese pay a heavy price for the priorities they have set. If, as most believe, there is "an underlying psychological malaise . . . it [comes] from the uniformity and strictness of the patterns society fixes on the individual" (Reischauer 1977: 230–1).

There are unmistakable signs that the priorities are shifting, however slowly. One of the findings of the successive studies of national character referred to above suggests the direction being taken. It is also one of the very few issues regarding which there is a marked generational shift. Among the responses to the question: "What kind of life do you want to live?" one of the choices is, "To live a life that suits one's own taste." Any given age cohort shows no change over the twenty years covered by these studies, but each succeeding, younger cohort makes the choice more frequently. The highest frequency is that registered in the 1973 survey by those born in the late 1950s, but even in this age group of twenty to twenty-four, only half express the preference (Hayashi 1975: 78; 1976). I will have more to say about the extent to which there appears to be a Japanese "generation gap" in the following chapter.

It has always seemed to me that the Japanese are very conscious of the way their society works and that they have shown great creativity and aptitude for change within the limits set for them by it. Yet by no means does everyone approve of the society they have fashioned, and there is a vast literature excoriating the contemporary Japanese for the kind of life they have chosen. They are accused of having embraced a mindless—or worse, a soulless—hedonistic consumerism, or are represented as the passive victims of, rather than consciously selective participants in, the productive system they have built. Taking exception to this view on behalf of another people, the late Anthony Crosland, then foreign secretary of the British Labour government, wrote of his working-class constituents words that seem to me very fitting in this context:

[They] want lower housing densities and better schools and hospitals. They want washing machines and refrigerators to relieve domestic drudgery. They want cars, and the freedom they give on weekends and holidays. And they want the package-tour holidays to Majorca, even if this means more noise of night flights and eat-

ing fish and chips on previously secluded beaches—why should they
too not enjoy the sun? And they want these things not . . . because
their minds have been brainwashed and their tastes contrived by
advertising, but because the things are desirable in themselves.[20]
Despite the chorus of despair of the social critics, who for
the most part write their pieces in air-conditioned rooms, take
their holidays in Guam, Hawaii, or Acapulco, and have at
hand a spectacular array of domestic appliances, the ordinary
Japanese has pursued analogous goals with such single-minded
devotion and with such evident self-satisfaction that in a recent
poll, 90 percent assigned themselves to the middle class. It will
not be long before the critics discover a memorable analysis
of the situation on Taiwan, now witnessing a similar con-
sumer boom. Seeking in vain to identify the malevolent agency
that has driven the evidently misguided masses to embrace
these new goals, one observer has characterized the phenomenon as "the self-exploitation of the petty bourgeoisie" (Gates
1979:397–402). It is an ingenious concept that probably applies to the Taiwanese case as little as it does to the Japanese.

In the final chapter I will examine the directions of change
in Japan in the postwar period in more detail, and try to show
that the Japanese bear a crushingly heavy burden, for they are
a people who in the last analysis believe that both the individual and society are perfectible.

4

The Perfectible Society

The least critical inquiry into the character of our civilization
in its present phase will show that the country is disfigured
by many imperfections and failings, which should be pointed
out specifically and which the nation must strive to correct.
Ōkuma Shigenobu 1910:II, 562.

In 1881 a foreign writer for a Yokohama English-language
newspaper looked editorially into his heavily overcast crystal
ball and wrote: "The Japanese are a happy race, and being
content with little, are not likely to achieve much."[1]

Almost a century later at least one bureaucrat in the European Common Market concluded in effect that the Japanese,
no longer content with little, had achieved entirely too much.
This view was expressed in a briefing document prepared for
the organization's external affairs commissioner, in Tokyo for
economic talks in the spring of 1979. Calling for consideration
of imposing limitations on Japanese exports, the author—the
widely held cynical view in Japan was that he could only have
been a Frenchman—discussed the basis for Japan's economic
success. He attributed it to a combination of hard work, discipline, company loyalty, and managerial ability, all of which is
accurate enough. Almost all Japanese would have concurred.
But there was more. Japan, the report continued, is "a land of
work maniacs who live in what . . . are hardly better than

106

rabbit hutches," and concluded with the following remarkable denunciation of Japanese values: "It is not easy [for us] to face competition from such a country, [for in] Europe the Protestant work ethic has been profoundly eroded by egalitarianism, social compassion, environmentalism, state intervention, and a widespread belief that to work hard and earn money is anti-social."[2]

Japanese editorialists roused themselves from a state of profound shock to express unbounded outrage. One cartoonist, borrowing an old song about an engaging ne'er-do-well, had one of his characters ask another: "Tell me, Mr. EC, why do you dislike Japan?" To which the second replied: "Because I like to nap, drink wine at lunch, and loaf around. That's why I don't like Japan." The refrain, sung by the first character, is: "Selfish! Selfish!"[3] Japanese friends began to issue wry invitations to come visit them in their rabbit hutches, but the Japanese government officially was not amused.

Levity aside, the shock was so profound, I think, because the report struck two very sensitive nerves. First, the Japanese routinely criticize themselves for working too hard, and know and resent the fact that in terms of living space they are by far the poorest industrial nation in the world. But beyond the shock of recognition was the reaction to the implied negative criticism of an achievement for which they had every right to expect to be admired. Once again Japan's emulation of the Western model as the Japanese understood it—imperialism in the late nineteenth and first half of the twentieth centuries, and economic growth in recent decades—had obviously aroused the hostility of the rest of the industrial world. For while Japan had slaved to catch up yet again, it now appeared that the West had quietly all but abandoned the model it had so recently provided. It is in their sense of betrayal that we must see a significant feature of the Japanese view of society as perfectible.

In Japanese utopian thinking, except for the brief interwar period of intense interest in utopian socialism, the model for the ideal society has been quite different from that with which we are familiar. The word "utopia" means "no place," but in the Japanese view the model for it is quite often thought to be some distant idealized country that must be emulated or surpassed (Nuita 1971:22).[4] Twice in earlier times the Japanese made China serve such a purpose, and twice in more recent history it was the idealized West to which they looked.

In the recent scholarly literature there has been waged a spirited debate over the issue of convergence of industrial systems toward a universal model. It is not my purpose to reconstruct the terms of that debate or even to deal in any formal way with the issues with which it is concerned. I have already made my position on the matter clear, and will simply rephrase it here. Although it is perfectly conceivable that a political regime can be overthrown in a very short period of time, as happened in Japan with the Tokugawa shogunate, it would be no small undertaking to destroy the values and attitudes shared by a people, even if one had the desire to do any such thing and all the time in the world (Nagashima 1973: 110).

It would nonetheless be foolish to maintain the position that Japanese values and attitudes are unchanging, but it is another question entirely as to whether they are becoming more and more like our own as the alleged convergence of the societies and cultures of the industrial states proceeds. Such claims frequently overlook not only the possibility of parallel developments, but more fatally usually have failed to consider the possibility that the attitudes and values of the peoples of all the industrial societies may themselves be changing and diverging. As times change, today's hot debate becomes tomorrow's dead issue. Rather than pursuing this particular line of argument, therefore, I will try instead to place the whole matter in a broader perspective and ask how the Japanese appear to think about the world and their place in it, and how they perceive their society.

It must never be forgotten that for most of their history, the Japanese have experienced only the most limited and intermittent contact with the people of other countries. They thus provide a highly unusual case of an isolated society that has assimilated many alien cultural elements—almost always on its own initiative—without directly meeting the producers of the adopted elements. The facts are well known, but what is not commonly remarked upon is that they have managed to remain quite complacent in the process (Ishida 1974: 113). That complacency is well grounded in Japanese myths.[5] "The earthly condition as men know it is presented . . . as all but universal. . . . Moreover, once the heavenly dynasty has taken possession of this world, there is little evidence that other regions of the cosmos can any longer have much effect on man's realm" (Pelzel 1970a: 43). The myths accord to the things of this world overwhelming priority and value, and contain no hint that "such cosmic forces as do exist can overpower life as man proposes to live it" (1970a: 44). Furthermore, "The natural world has life and will that are all but identical with those of man," and in this connection it is significant that Japan's culture heroes had as their primary task to deprive plants and inorganic objects of the qualities of speech, mobility, and violence that they originally possessed (1970a: 47). "The universe conforms to worldly and human experiences and provides no more justification to the fatalist than [to the optimist]. Events oscillate fairly evenly about a mean that for man as a whole is life-sustaining." And although Buddhism was later to provide a keen sense of the unattainable and ample grounds for the fear of death, "One senses that in the mythic view it is the fate of mankind to succeed" (1970a: 48) through the exertion of a reasonable amount of effort. This is a pleasant vision of the Japanese construction of these matters, but it may underestimate the amount of effort that is judged to be reasonable. Kurt Singer (1973: 95) thought that "Japan has to offer few contributions to world culture except this signal one: to have given an example of a style of life subordinating everything to one value: duration." And, we might well add, endurance.

No examination of the ways in which the Japanese perceive themselves and their society would be complete without reference to the strong tendency on their part to define it and themselves as unique. The production of books and essays on what may be called Japan-ism and Japanese-ism (*nihonron* and *nihonjinron*, respectively) has in recent years assumed the status of a thriving cottage industry. The quality of most of this outpouring is rather poor, but even the best of it is calculated to irritate or infuriate the comparativist,[6] for the argument is not just that the Japanese "way of thinking" is unusual or different in degree from that of other peoples, but rather that it is totally unlike them. Nowhere is the character of this viewpoint more clearly epitomized than in discussions of Japanese rationality or lack thereof. Consider the following statements made in recent years by three men of very different background and training:

. . . [T]he Japanese do not emphasize the European logical premises which claim to classify and categorize objects. The Japanese mode of thought does not set up classifications and categories such as good and evil, self and other, man and nature, or life and death with which to structure concepts. Consequently . . . logic and rhetoric did not develop in Japan. (Ishida 1974: 117)

. . . [R]ationalism is a pattern of thinking which inquires into everything in the background of an ensemble of complementary possibilities. The peculiarity of the Japanese mode of thinking lies in its complete neglect of complementary alternatives. [There is a] tendency to sidestep as far as possible any kind of confrontation.

This, in turn, leads to the tendency to retain the existing stability with the least amount of modification at the sacrifice of a thoroughgoing solution. [There is also a tendency] to avoid any form of rational compromise based on a selection from among alternative possibilities. . . . Japanese thought is concerned mainly [with] the local and temporary order restricted in space and time. (Yukawa 1967: 54–6)

Any adequate discussion of the status of the individual and of the relationship between the individual and the universal in Japanese thought and culture . . . requires an examination of two major aspects of the problem—the philosophical or linguistic and the logical, that is, the tendency toward an absence of theoretical or systematic thinking, along with an emphasis upon an aesthetic and intuitive and concrete, rather than a strictly logical orientation. (Nakamura 1968: 141)

It may be regarded as a rather serious matter for anyone to charge that the Japanese are not concerned with logical distinctions or the exclusivity of complementary alternatives. Were a foreigner to do so, he would surely be branded a racist or worse. Yet the authors of these three passages are all Japanese, and they have reached their shared conclusion by very different routes. The first is by Ishida Eiichirō, one of the most distinguished ethnologists of the twentieth century; the second by Yukawa Hideki, winner of the Nobel prize for physics; the third by Nakamura Hajime, renowned philosopher and student of the history of religion. All three write in the same vein for Japanese audiences. One may agree or disagree with their position, but whether it is correct or even conceivable is beside the point, for it is undeniably a datum in its own right. Why should any people wish to hear, as the Japanese apparently do on the evidence of the enormous sales of books making the point, that they cannot or do not or will not think logically?

One plausible answer is that the claim is only a way of

saying to foreigners that they will never understand the Japanese because they think differently. Viewed in this light, it serves as a powerful device for explaining away misperception and misunderstanding as inevitable outcomes of interaction between themselves and other peoples. Alternatively, it may be only one of the many ways in which the Japanese phrase their awful sense of isolation from the rest of the world, although the claim is not without an element of perverse pride. And finally—and even to suggest the possibility is to run the risk of rousing the ire of those who are repelled by the very thought—it is just conceivable that the authors are right. Perhaps, after all the international experience they gained in dealing with other peoples, these men are simply saying there is evidence around them in their daily lives that at the very least suggests their compatriots are not much preoccupied with assessing the right and wrong or good and bad of things on the basis of abstract principles—that they are not, after all, "reason freaks."

For the Tokugawa ideologues of the School of National Learning, the golden age lay in the remote past. In this, if in little else, they concurred with the neo-Confucianists, who differed only in that they thought it lay in the remote Chinese past. The members of the School of National Learning believed that order in the present could best be maintained in the absence of innovation. In the eighteenth century Motoori Norinaga, one of the greatest of them, wrote: "Even things that are profitable, if they are of a new form, are customarily to be considered troublesome; and for this reason, things that are traditional, even though containing slight elements of harm, for the most part should remain as they are."[7] Among the neo–Confucian scholars of that period as well, whose thought was severely circumscribed by a world view almost completely hierarchic in character, "there were exceedingly few men who were willing to seek, or even felt the need for,

alternatives to the traditional principles. . . . For scholars and
activists alike, knowledge still responded to the calls of an
insular society requiring ever-renewed affirmation of inherited
values" (Miyoshi 1979: 122). The high price paid for this
orientation to the world has been "the conspicuous absence
of the speculative habit of mind," for the Japanese have
chosen instead "to forego universalistic knowledge, skeptical
observation, and individual reflection in order to sustain a
close and coherent community inherited from the long past."[8]

Yet as I have repeatedly stressed, for all its inclinations and
preferences, Japanese thought (the neo–Confucian variety included) was intensely pragmatic and "by no means a deterrent
to other kinds of learning. If it was not exactly charged with
the humanistic spirit, it nonetheless taught a reverence for
learning in general; if free inquiry was not its first principle . . .
it allowed the student to interpret the Way of the Sages as he
saw it; and if group consciousness was dominant, it yet encouraged competition within the group" (Miyoshi 1979: 124).
Perhaps this dual attitude has much to do with the general
lack of concern for apparent contradictions between theory
and practice.[9]

The theme of competition within the group is one that has
been explored by many scholars. Robert Bellah (1957) has
argued that in the values of the Tokugawa period, particularism rather than universalism held primacy, and the chief concern was for the achievement of the goals of the system rather
than mere maintenance of the system itself. Loyalty, a particularistic tie to the head of one's collectivity, was therefore
accorded the status rather than the person. Since the concern
was primarily with system goals, performance was elevated to
the position of a primary value. Status alone did not validate;
it was performance in the pursuit of system goals that was
ultimately validating. The concept of reciprocal responsibility
has long characterized the relationship between leader and

follower, as it continues to do today. Loyalty in Japan has never meant merely passive devotion. Competition in performance is therefore a feature of all groups that comprise such a system. Furthermore, as we have seen, collective responsibility of all for the actions of any member of the group is assumed, and a higher priority is given public interest than individual rights.

The history of the development of contemporary Japanese society is charged with the conflicts between these underlying postulates and the myriad challenges to them occasioned by the opening of Japan at the end of the nineteenth century. From 1868 to 1945, tensions flared into intermittent outbursts of violence that threw into increasingly sharp relief the severe strains the system was experiencing. To preserve its control, the government employed the twin techniques of intensive indoctrination through the compulsory educational system and the military services on the one hand, and outright repression of dissidents on the other. Increasingly conservative, it was paying at least one high price for its success that the early Meiji leaders apparently had foreseen and had taken as an acceptable risk. Because the state they built rested on an assertion of a monopoly on morality, one consequence of their successful rout of the liberal forces had been to leave the whole system vulnerable in a very special way. It is of immense significance that all the failed coups d'état of Japan's modern century have come from the right in the name of that purest of motives, imperial loyalty. It was that same, by then anachronistic, motivation that in 1970 impelled the novelist Mishima to his bloody end. Like the rebel Saigō Takamori in the 1870s and the Young Officers of the coup of 1936, Mishima believed Japan's future lay in the reaffirmation of the timeless values associated with the only true embodiment of the essence of the Japanese state and its people.

Mishima's disastrous miscalculation led him to act with

total propriety, but in the wrong version of Japanese society, for the catastrophic end of the Greater East Asia War had exploded forever the carefully contrived blend of myth and history, the appeals to adopt Western technology in the context of Japanese values, and the chauvinism so successfully fostered by the system of public education. Ironically, it was the voice of the emperor himself, heard for the first time by his subjects, that dealt the system the coup de grace, albeit in terms with fascinating resonances. In a radio broadcast on August 15, 1945, expressing his profound sorrow for their suffering, he said in part:

... [I] t is according to the dictates of time and fate that we have resolved to pave the way for a grand peace for all the generations to come by enduring the unendurable and suffering what is insufferable.... Let the entire nation continue as one family from generation to generation, ever firm in its faith in the imperishability of this divine land ... mindful of its heavy burden of responsibilities, and the long road before it. Unite your total strength to be devoted to construction for the future. Cultivate the ways of rectitude and nobility of spirit, and work with resolution so that you may enhance the innate glory of the Imperial State and keep pace with the progress of the world.[10]

His grandfather, the Meiji emperor, would have approved the sentiments wholeheartedly, but his subjects responded less to them than to the exigencies of the time with such single-minded earnestness and with such a degree of success that it was a scant generation later that they stood accused of perversity in their unconscionable adherence to the spirit of the Protestant ethic!

Those who accomplished that miracle of recovery were the grandparents and parents of today's youth. What, then, of the young? Fully 60 percent of all living Japanese were born after the surrender, and we may well wonder to what extent the postwar generations share anything with their elders, who rebuilt their shattered lives and tried to keep pace with the progress of the world. All the evidence is that they share quite a bit more than may be apparent on the surface. William Cummings (1980: 196–7) makes the point more explicitly than any other commentator on the educational system that I know.

The various pieces of information do suggest that contemporary youths have developed a new orientation to life that is more inward looking and less concerned with extrinsic rewards and social achievement. Although this new tendency is labeled here as emerging individuated orientation, this may lead to some misunderstanding. Unquestionably today's young people are more concerned about personal growth and satisfaction and hence are more individualistic. On the other hand, this does not mean that they reject group life or avoid involvement in large collectivities. To the contrary, today's young people appear just as positive as ever about group life. They mention love and friendship as among the values they consider most important. They enjoy school club activities and other opportunities for collective endeavor, such as school trips. And as they move into work, most mention relations with coworkers and bosses as a major personal concern. Thus, the new individualism does not mean a rejection of taking part in groups; rather, it seems to involve a new orientation to the group. The group is viewed as a collection of individuals, each of whom is seeking self-fulfillment. A group is appreciated insofar as it is responsive to individual needs. In contrast, a group that imposes rigid and non-negotiable demands on its individual members is disliked. One can see how this contingent view of group life relates to the . . . new skepticism toward authority and established politics.

Robert Cole reports that young workers take up employment filled with high ideals of the very sort he believes were held by their parents and grandparents before them: "The cultural values inherited from the Meiji period which emphasized the importance of making Japan a modern industrial country are easily adapted to contemporary demands for higher wages and better working conditions . . . or to political action for social reform. There are also the persisting historic values expressed in the concept of [striving for success] which results in children being taught in the family that 'you have to be better than we are' " (1971: 157). These are not merely abstract ideals, but directly affect the behavior of the young workers who hold them. "They are willing to unite, sacrifice, and take risks to achieve these ideals. Worker solidarity is strong in their early years" (ibid.), but their ideals are not those of political and industrial social democracy. They focus instead on higher wages, shorter hours, and an even chance of being promoted according to ability rather than having to wait out the seniority system of advancement. Their energies are considerable, and management stands ever ready to harness them in ways not at all familiar to most Americans.

As Dore (1973:401–2) has pointed out, at the onset of Japan's industrial development in the late nineteenth century, "the modified Confucian world-view [meant that those in] positions of authority . . . have been rather less disposed than their Western counterparts to see their subordinates as donkeys responsive to sticks and carrots, and more disposed to see them as human beings responsive to moral agents," for Japanese Confucianism assumes original virtue rather than original sin.[11] The presumed responsiveness to moral agents has led management to indulge in the lavish use of slogans and company insignia, and to make unremitting efforts through ritual and ceremony to promote a sense of common enterprise—of system goals, in fact (Dore 1973: 23–4; Rohlen 1974: 34–61). It is that sense of common enterprise that so strikes American businesspeople and managerial personnel about what they see in Japanese companies and plants. One of them said to me, shortly after his return from his first visit to Japan: "I had always been taught that conflict between management and labor is inevitable. I've now seen a place where the two seem actually to think they are working together to achieve a shared goal!"

In the light of the foregoing, it is fascinating to discover that among the very few features of the Japanese industrial system in which Cole finds some prospect for profitable borrowing by Americans, who lack it, is the kind of policy that successfully unites personal and organizational goals, recognizing the legitimacy of the former and responding to them, while always assigning ultimate priority to the latter.[12] Most Americans will wonder whether or not younger workers really buy the formula. Earlier I referred to studies which show that the expression of preference for a boss endowed with the virtues of humaneness and sympathy (*ninjō*) has held, with the exception of the 1958 survey, at around 82 to 85 percent throughout the twenty years during which the national character surveys have been conducted. What is remarkable is that within that consistent percentage throughout the period, it is the younger age groups that select it with the highest frequency (Dore 1973: 237).[13]

Perhaps no aspect of the world of work in Japan has excited more interest than that of permanent employment or lifetime commitment, yet the concept is often misunderstood (Clark 1979). Care must be taken to disassemble the several meanings of the term used to describe the phenomenon. First, there is the normative meaning, which refers to the moral obligation of the employer to retain the services of the worker who is hired. It is management that makes the commitment, not the employee, who theoretically is free to change jobs if he or she wishes to do so. The issue is not whether workers actually stay with the same firm for life, and there is ample evidence to show that many do not. Nevertheless, the employer does expect the people hired to stay with the firm until they retire, and Clark offers convincing evidence that workers have a sense of obligation to do just that, or at the very least that they initially take up employment in the clear expectation that they will do so. In the company he studied, Clark found that workers of all ages viewed the concept of lifetime commitment as both normal and right, and saw the worker and the firm bound in a reciprocal relationship of enduring mutual interest. The concept of lifetime commitment represents, then, "an ideal, and a very powerful one, entailing an obligation of mutual attachment between firm and employee. Sanctioned by what [both see] as tradition, morally correct, and emblematic of Japanese culture, 'lifetime commitment' is the goal towards which both firms and individuals have to direct their efforts" (1979: 175). Therefore, when an employee does resign before scheduled retirement, there is a ready explanation for his behavior. "Put briefly, it is that no one would normally join a company unless to stay in it, so that if a man does leave, then there must be some defect in the company or in the man himself. . . . [Furthermore] people believed that the company *ought* to be a community," and they tried very hard to make it so (1979: 200).

That attitude is shared by the employers, and perhaps more important, by the government, which heavily subsidizes firms in periods of economic downturn to help them keep employees who in the United States would simply be thrown out into the streets in hard times (Cole 1979: 256–7). This hardly disinterested policy clearly reveals a sensible assessment of the high psychological and social costs, not to mention the political danger, of allowing unemployment to rise sharply in times of economic decline. It is apparent that government and business share the view that the employment practice in question is a major key to industrial and societal harmony. So do the regular male employees in Japanese industry and commerce to whom in fact it chiefly applies, perhaps half to two-thirds of the male labor force, and these include the young as well as the old.

They do disagree on many things, but it is very hard to see that a chasm has opened up between them. In the 1968 national character survey, for example, respondents were asked whether they would assign higher priority to individual rights or public interest. Those over sixty years of age were inclined to opt for the public interest (but still only 62 percent of them did so), whereas about half of those aged twenty to twenty-four made that choice.[14] What is rather surprising, therefore, is the virtual impossibility of finding a living Japanese over the age of, say, forty-five who doubts the existence of a severe malaise among the alienated young, who are themselves much given to its public expression.

What, then, shall we make of the repeated findings that the young do not diverge significantly from adults in their endorsement of the importance of family ties, even when they are responding to such traditional stimuli as attitudes toward filial piety? Lebra's (1974: 272) guess is that there is alienation aplenty, but that it is alienation from social units larger than or outside the conjugal family, now overwhelmingly the most common residential form of the family in Japan. She suggests that the positive identification with the family may stem chiefly from their prolonged and almost exclusive dependence on it. She is, I think, quite right about the importance of the conjugal family to today's youth, but as we have seen they appear to continue to assign considerable importance to other kinds of group affiliation as well.

One of the most striking features of postwar demography has been the absolute and proportionate increase in the number of conjugal families in Japan, coupled with divorce rates that are among the lowest in the industrial world. Traditionalists view with alarm the growing tendency for young married couples to retreat into what is given the engaging name of "my-home-ism."[15] Today young men are said by their older superiors in the company to devote too much time to the domestic unit; it was not long ago, after all, that a man might be stigmatized as an *aisaika*, literally a "wife lover." The implied criticism, of course, was that as a consequence of this defect of character he devoted less time and attention to his work-related responsibilities than his employers could reasonably expect of him. Now, however, young couples and their children may be seen on Sunday outings and holidays together, something almost never observed even twenty years ago, and there is great emphasis on the acquisition of a house or apartment, domestic appliances, and a family car (called, appropriately enough, "my-car")—all in the name of creating a bright "my-home."

To the extent that this preoccupation signals a weakening of ties to the performance-oriented work group, it is interpreted by many as a sign of the decline of community, hierarchy, authority, and social responsibility. It may well be so, and if it is the case, it is almost the only aspect of change in postwar Japan that can be attributed even indirectly to the changing role of women. For the rise of my-home-ism and the privatization of life corresponds exactly to the rise within the conjugal family of the power of young wives (Kiefer 1976: 292), whose main loyalty is to it alone, rather than to any larger social grouping, such as the husband's household or any other more extensive kin group.

The rise of the conjugal family has had other effects as well. With the eradication from the curricula of the primary and middle schools of the pre-1945 courses on ethics and morals, most of the responsibility for that kind of instruction of the young fell on the family by default. Very many Japanese were of the opinion that this new family simply was not up to the job, and called for the reintroduction of such materials in the classroom (R. J. Smith 1978: 181–2). Unless the educational system once again took charge of these matters, they maintained, what was already a bad situation would only grow

progressively worse. It hardly need be said that powerful conservative political elements endorse this sentiment wholeheartedly, but it is less widely recognized that the powerful Japan
Teacher's Union (Nikkyōso) has pursued a highly successful
effort to introduce into the hours now set aside for moral instruction material of distinctly "progressive" content (Cummings 1980: 115–18). They do not disagree with the government over the principle that the schools are appropriate places
for such instruction, but the two differ sharply on what kind
of morality shall be taught. To date the situation remains at
an impasse.

Thus we may safely assume that young people in Japan in
fact do not acquire their values and attitudes exclusively from
their elders in the context of the family. Cole has remarked
that there now exists segregation of older youth on an unprecedented scale by virtue of the rapid expansion of the educational system since the end of the war. Over half of all college
and university students are in Tokyo or Osaka, and most of
them are living away from home. "The significance of the
accelerated process of youth segregation and concentration is
that youths come to be influenced more by peer groups than
by the values and behavior of their elders" (1976: 201). The
implication is that such a situation provides fertile ground for
the rapid development of new values and attitudes in the
absence of firm guidance by the parental generation. Although
Cole acknowledges it is the scale rather than the practice of
youth segregation that is new, there is reason nonetheless to
believe there is an essential continuity that seems to me to
argue for a constancy of values transmission. It was Kurt Singer
(1973: 34) who remarked on what he called a peculiar trait of
Japanese upbringing he had observed in the 1930s. It seemed
to him remarkable the extent to which "discipline and con-
straint, at least during their decisive stages, are imposed [on
the young] less from outside, by men of greater age [and]

authority, than by members of their own age group," who in that period were the segregated youth of the middle and higher schools, and therefore younger than today's university students.[16]

As to the constancy of the transmission of values, I should think it clear that among the young, peer pressures to conform to group norms are demonstrably more formidable than those liable to be imposed by parents, whose disciplinary actions are likely to be tempered by a measure of love. There is also good reason to believe that the young socialize one another to values and attitudes considerably more authoritarian and doctrinaire in character than most of us would like to believe. The remaining question, then, is do the norms of the two age groups differ substantially? In Japan today, despite the grave misgivings of members of the older age groups, I think the answer is "no," for the structural constraints on the exercise of individual initiative and optative behavior remain firmly grounded in the objective conditions of the real world, the society the Japanese have built.

There is an assumption widely shared at all levels of Japanese society and among all age groups that gives this chapter its title, although it is seldom so explicitly phrased. As we have seen, the individual is urged to strive for perfection.[17] If individuals attain that goal, then society, being the creation of individuals, is itself perfectible. The assumption derives from the premise, deeply rooted in native myth, Confucian teachings,[18] and the peculiar construction the Japanese have placed on Buddhism, that human beings have this world and this life and none other. If there is a conception of immortality, it is lodged squarely in the practice of the ancestral rites of the household. The head of a household has as one of his important duties to make certain there is a successor in the generation after his. The injunction to secure the succession has heavy and sacred overtones. A person's spirit is sustained by his descendants, and although in theory Buddhism holds out the hope of individual salvation, it has been thought for centuries that the care of the souls of the dead is chiefly the responsibility of those they have left behind in this world. The spirits of the deceased delight in the success of their descendants, are fed by their hands the same food eaten by the living, and are linked to their households eternally through proper observance of the memorial rites. As Plath (1964), ever ready with an apt aphorism, has put it, in Japan the Family of God is the family.

In this world the living bear the heavy burden of an unre-payable debt to the collectivity of the ancestors who gave them life, and each must strive to contribute what he or she can to the patrimony of those who will come after. Human nature, essentially good, is nevertheless such that individuals must discipline themselves to meet the demands of society. So far, at least, the Japanese have elected to forego the asser-tion of the right to the expression of untrammeled personal freedom in the interest of the maintenance of public order and the service of the common good.

Indeed, the drive to reestablish public order as well as personal integrity has been a central concern of the national effort in the entire postwar period. Nowhere is its success more evident than in the remarkable achievement with respect to the control of violent crime.[19] Tokyo has no more police per capita than New York City, and both are densely crowded and vast in scale—yet in terms of their rates of major crime, the two places could hardly be more different. A few figures will suffice to show the dimensions of that difference. In 1977 for every 100,000 people, there were 20.8 murders in New York, 1.7 in Tokyo; New York had 994 robberies, Tokyo 3.1; there were 6,525 burglaries in New York, 576 in Tokyo. Only in the rate of assaults on the person do the two cities come even close: 562 to 148. The contrast is stunning, but it is not central to my purpose to compare our two societies. The extraordinary thing about the Japanese figures is that they represent either substantial declines since the 1950s or at worst a steady rate over the past twenty-odd years. It should not be forgotten that it is in that very time span that the massive migration of the rural population to the cities of Japan has occurred.

Accompanying the stability or decline in rates of violent crime is the successful transformation of the public's perception of the police from that of occasionally brutal, usually harsh figures of authority accorded respect largely based on fear to one of a very different kind. It is today the assumption of the vast majority of Japanese that police and public alike are on the same side in the unremitting effort to maintain order and minimize the dangers encountered by ordinary people in the conduct of their daily lives. Police behavior has improved immeasurably over the past thirty-five years, as is suggested by the astonishing fact that the number of complaints lodged against them with the civilian review boards of the Ministry of Justice has declined annually since their establishment in 1948 to the present level of about one hundred a year, this in a population of about 116 million.

Police scandal is virtually unknown, and the rate of arrests per number of crimes known to the police—the so-called clearance rate—is the highest in the industrial world. This achievement is only partly the result of good police work, as they themselves are the first to admit. Far more directly it stems from their successful efforts to enlist the cooperation of the public, which is urged to report suspicious individuals, odd circumstances, and unusual events, and from the pattern of dispersal throughout all cities of small police boxes, from which no resident who may need help is very far, and which are staffed around the clock. The police have pursued a highly successful campaign of organizing citizen's groups, commonly based on neighborhood associations already in existence. They present themselves as basically service-oriented, and provide counseling and guidance on a wide range of problems either in person or by telephone. Twice a year someone from the local police box calls at every dwelling and place of business to update the record of who lives or works there. Few refuse to supply the information on the grounds that its collection represents an invasion of privacy.

The public also backs the authorities in the stringent control of handguns, a policy so effective that for any recent year's reported 80,000-odd major crimes in Tokyo, guns figure in no more than 20. The only legal handguns aside from those issued to the police are in the possession of members of the Olympic shooting team. The police, who still prefer not to carry their sidearms even when on riot duty, unsuccessfully resisted the American decision to arm them during the Occupation period, arguing that such a step would serve them ill. The correctness of their assumption is demonstrated by the contrast between our two societies with respect to police fatalities. In 1973, of the 127 police officers killed in the line of duty in the United States, 125 died from gunshot wounds. During the four-year period 1969–72, 16 Japanese police officers were killed, 3 of them the victims of firearms.

Narcotics abuse was a severe problem in Japan throughout the 1950s. Despite recent increases over the low figures of the past two decades, it remains at levels guaranteed to excite the envy or disbelief of American law enforcement authorities. Again the public strongly approves of the policy of strict enforcement of the narcotics laws, as they do of gun control, on the entirely reasonable grounds that no one's interests are well served by condoning or encouraging the spread of either. What the postwar history of Japan shows most clearly, perhaps, is that it is possible for a people to act effectively on the assumption that crime, far from being an inevitable consequence of urbanization and industrialization, is susceptible to control through social engineering. And lest it be assumed that harshness of punishment is a factor in discouraging criminal activity, let me report that in 1973 only about 5 percent of those convicted of a crime were actually given prison terms, compared to 45 percent in the United States. The result is that in Japan there is a small prison population—believed by most Japanese to represent a true criminal element—and a larger number of persons who have only been fined and returned to society.

Two factors of critical importance in the decline of rates of major crime in postwar Japan are the economic situation, which might readily be predicted, and one aspect of the structure of Japanese society, which will be less obvious to the Western reader. The proposition relating to the first of these can be stated simply: Rapid secular growth in economic opportunities contributes to a reduction in criminal activity The Japanese case appears to bear out this proposition, for during the postwar years the high rate of economic growth has indeed been accompanied by a dramatic decline in the rate of violent crime, as we have seen. One stipulation must be made, however. In the prewar years, rates of economic growth and violent crime did not covary, suggesting that the inverse relationship between the two obtains only when significant and sustained economic growth is maintained, as has been the case since the 1950s (Evans 1977: 486).

As for the social factor referred to above, it seems clear that the intense identification of the individual with small groups of affiliation has been of critical importance in the decline of crime rates in the postwar period. Most Japanese believe that one's actions will reflect on one's group, although its members no longer pay any legal penalty for the transgressions of the offender among them, as they once did. The intensity of identification is manifested in many ways in the most mundane as well as in highly dramatic contexts. In the winter of 1979, when television camera crews attempted to film ordinary office workers arriving at their company on the morning following the suicide of a vice-president who had assumed blame for company involvement in a major bribery scandal, all shielded their faces or turned and bolted out of camera range. The taint of scandal was felt to affect them all and there was no question of allowing themselves to be interviewed, for it would have been disloyal in the extreme to comment to any outsider on the disaster that had cast discredit on the whole enterprise.

Some weeks later the television news carried an interview with a man who appeared to be in his forties, who had become something of a media hero. He had been working at a construction site near a small branch post office that was held up by a youth wielding a knife. The youth had fled, with the post office employees in hot pursuit, and as he ran past, the construction worker tackled him and wrestled him to the ground. When the police arrived to make the arrest, the man discovered for the first time that the robber was armed. The media were intent on showing the public a man who had got involved, and the reporter asked him what his reaction had been when he saw the knife. His reply is paradigmatic of a general attitude, as I discovered when I asked several people about it: "I just automatically grabbed him when I heard those people shouting to stop him. What would I have done if I'd known he had a knife? I'm not so sure now, because now I realize that I might have got hurt and had to take time off from my job. How could I ever have explained that to my company?"

There are in daily life many less dramatic occasions on which the power of group affiliation is demonstrated, but suffice it to say that if I am correct in thinking it plays a central role in producing the orderly society that contemporary Japan has become, it follows that these groups must have *strength-*

ened their hold over the individual in the postwar period as
traditional hierarchies have weakened or collapsed. Furthermore, there can be no doubt that to a quite remarkable degree
the values of the total system remain embedded in each relatively self-contained group, and that the smooth functioning
of each plays an indispensable part in the preservation of the
total structure. Japan is, of course, no longer a Confucian
state in any formal sense, but the sentiment expressed in the
Analects that I have already quoted is germane to the issue
at hand: "Their persons being cultivated, their families were
regulated. Their families being regulated, their states were
rightly governed."

This perception of the nature of the social order produces
at least two great problems, however. The first is that its
emphasis on self-cultivation may well result in an almost total
lack of what we in the West would call civic consciousness.
This has been so much the case in Japan that concern is expressed on every hand, and much effort expended by reform
groups, civic-minded organizers, and sometimes even the government itself to appeal for improvement in the quality of
public behavior. It is of some interest that despite, or perhaps
because of, the availability of a very large lexicon dealing with
traditional norms of behavior, propriety, etiquette, and the
like, those concerned to promote more civil deportment have
taken up the English word "manners" instead. At major inter-
sections, for example, one sees large signboards bearing slogans
and admonitions such as *Kōtsū manā: jibun dake wa to omou
tokoro ga jiko no moto* (Traffic Manners: Accidents happen
when you think only of yourself). Should any of my readers
imagine that the Japanese never think of the self or display
self-interest, they need only drive an automobile in that country, preferably at the rush hour on a major highway.

The distinction between public and private, which in the
West is ultimately connected with that between church and

state, cannot exist where the state itself is conceived to be a moral entity. Prior to the Greater East Asia War, the Japanese state never pretended to derive its authority from morally neutral, external laws. Instead, it based its control on the creation of a system of internal values, inculcated in its citizenry through its educational and military institutions.

Although much has changed in the postwar period, there persists strong popular support for the proposition that the proper place for ethical instruction remains the public school classroom. The unrelenting opposition of the Japan Teacher's Union to government efforts to reintroduce conservative courses of this kind into the curriculum, as we have seen, does not reflect its rejection of the idea—the issue is only the content of the courses. The state today is deprived of its erstwhile monopoly on morality and the household lacks its former authority over the individual, yet there is no church or any other analogous institution invested with the moral character that once inhered in the state. It is one of the ironies of the postwar period that the political right and left are agreed that the only possible recourse is to the system of public education.

The second problem raised by the Confucian formulation cited above is that of dissent and its control. I have touched only occasionally on the question of nonconformity and dissidence, and the ways in which they are expressed and attempts made to counteract them. One of the consequences of the nature of the Japanese polity is that the powerless and the socially inferior suffer a cruel handicap. Unable to forge durable links based on common interest or socioeconomic class, they remain at the mercy of those who wield political power in the name of moral rectitude (Nakane 1970: 150).[20] The situation makes for efficiency in performance, but it is potentially a source of danger. Despite all the constraints, there are labor disputes and strikes, contending political parties—factions is probably the better word—to right and left of center, and there is violence (Najita and Koschmann 1982; Sugimoto 1980). There are ad hoc groups formed to protest environmental pollution, inadequate housing, the corruption rampant in both business and government; and there are the Japanese Red Army, the organized opponents of the Narita International Airport, and groups of all kinds that from time to time take to the streets in massive outpourings of protest against the policies of those in power, or their heedlessness.

Some seek redress, some revolution. The first tend to call on the authorities to return to the path of virtue; the second, finding the authorities iniquitous beyond redemption, offer themselves as their virtuous replacements. What is noteworthy is the frequently convulsive nature of the upheavals, resulting without a doubt from the tendency of members of this society to suppress grievances and dissatisfaction for long periods of time. Almost as striking is the total inability to heal certain kinds of breaches between the authorities and dissident groups. One such breach deserves our attention for the light it sheds on the tendency of the system as I have described it to break down when either party to a dispute proves intransigent.

For more than seven long years, the government of Japan failed in its efforts to open the completed facilities at the new Narita International Airport (Anonymous 1978). In operation at last, it remains today an armed camp, ringed by a high fence that separates its constant police patrols from the entrenched protesters, a complex group of farmers, students, and antigovernment activists of many kinds. In the intermittent bloody pitched battles between the riot police and the protesters over the seven years, more than 8,000 were treated for injuries. Five died, four of them police officers, eloquent testimony that those who wield authority in postwar Japan have no sense it is the right of the state to take the lives of its citizens, however violent the form of their protest against its policies. As in the program to reform the police, we find here evidence of a

marked shift, for the prewar Japanese state, far less committed
to such humane principles, dealt with its dissident subjects
very harshly indeed.

At Narita, the impasse appears to be total. It stems directly
from the initial failure of the government to conduct the kind
of lengthy negotiations with local landowners that would have
required far fewer than seven years to reach a compromise
that would have led inevitably to agreement.[21] It is now too
late, for the possibility of establishing mutual trust is irredeem-
ably lost, as is the prospect of the government's bringing to
bear the amount of force it surely possesses to put an end to
the standoff. There exists no basis for conciliation or compromise, and all parties to the dispute have predictably long
since resorted to the courts, where the case is likely to be for
the indefinite future.

Protest is by no means a new phenomenon in Japan.
Throughout the Tokugawa period there is ample demonstra-
tion of dissatisfaction and discontent.[22] Response to these protests was, as I have suggested earlier, only as humane and
even-handed as those who administered the system of justice.
When groups in the society felt themselves sufficiently abused
by irresponsible or inept figures of authority, they conceived
they had the right to seek redress from still more highly placed
authorities—or, if they had no sense of rights, they knew such
a course was the only option available to them. Peasant re-
volts are a centerpiece of the history of conflict in Japan, and
many popular heroes of the old commoner classes of the Tokugawa period are men who led efforts to call to account immoral
authorities whose behavior they felt violated principles essential to the operation of the system.

A common but by no means exclusive pattern of rebellion
was one in which the leaders of the protest bypassed the
proximate figure of authority in the hierarchy—the village
headman or the local magistrate—and presented a petition at

a higher level. Their goal, often a reduction of rents in time of hardship, was always specific and limited in scope. To an astonishing extent these protests were effective, perhaps because they so often took as their targets those who by any lights were maladministering their local areas of responsibility. When such individuals were exposed, it was equally in the interest of the higher authorities and the peasants to remove them, install new personnel, and restore less ruinous conditions in the countryside. But the system could not really countenance the deliberate flouting of authority, with the result that the leaders of the rebellions—successful and unsuccessful alike—were routinely sentenced to death. The use of circular signatures on petitions to conceal the identity of the leaders was one response to this draconian policy.[23] Indifferent to the justice of their cause, the authorities meted out punishment that confirmed the validity of the premises on which their exercise of power was based. It could not be permitted that one go beyond local and immediate authority and fail to suffer the consequences.

Today, it need hardly be said, the world is very different. Yet a close look at the new citizens' protest movements in Japan strongly suggests that they remain largely centered on the community or neighborhood group and deal with a single, local issue.[24] Neither urban or rural protest groups show any tendency to link up into larger-scale organizations or to take on a range of issues. Their goals are usually the correction of a condition they believe to have arisen through irresponsible policies or inept performance procedures, or the prevention of a development they define as threatening to the community and the welfare of its residents. Almost all employ a rhetoric that urges the authorities to provide what the protesters believe to be fair and just treatment. When, as at Narita, both sides define the other as unresponsive to appeals for responsible behavior, there can easily develop situations in which there literally is no way left to resolve the issue, for neither party is

susceptible to any moral pressures the other might attempt to
bring to bear.

In such cases, the public's reaction by and large is to condemn them both for each in its own way having failed to
steer a course between self-interest and concern for the common good that would have led to a mutually satisfactory outcome in which, be it not forgotten, both sides would have
lost something.[25] The public's special impatience with the
situation at Narita stems in part from a recognition of the deep
irony with which it is tinged. In what is perhaps the most
tranquil of all industrial societies, rent by no religious, language, racial, or major ethnic schisms, the main international
airport is so vulnerable to violence that the planes of visiting
heads of state are not permitted to land there. They use instead the old facilities of Haneda Airport in Tokyo, from
which they may be conveyed safely to their destinations in
the city.

Most Japanese wish it were otherwise, for peace and harmony seem to them preferable to conflict and disorder. So do
they to most people of most societies, not least the Americans.
It must nevertheless seem to us that in their concern to maintain social order, the Japanese have too thoroughly discouraged
the open expression of individuality, in which we are likely to
see the ultimate strength of any social system. The Japanese,
with equal certainty, are likely to feel that the Americans
have so inflated the importance of the private self that we
run the risk of dissolving the bonds that must exist in order
to hold any human society together (Barnlund 1975: 171).

Lest we mistakenly imagine that this perception of the
character of the two societies is newly arrived at or reflects only
recent developments, let it be noted that well over one
hundred years ago a visitor to Japan wrote:

It is a singular fact, that in Japan, where the individual is sacrificed
to the community, he should seem perfectly happy and contented;

while in America, where exactly the opposite result takes place, and the community is sacrificed to the individual, the latter is in a perpetual state of uproarious clamor for his rights. (Oliphant 1860: 393)

Despite that fundamentally different orientation, upon a little reflection it is difficult to disagree with the suggestion that "there is no inherent reason why industrial progress cannot be directed toward utopian, communalistic goals," in Japan (Bikle 1971: 39), rather than increasing individual autonomy. The danger is that if the utopian goal is nothing more than to improve the conditions of daily life, the outcome may degenerate into an obsessive search for efficiency to the exclusion of all else. The danger of other kinds of utopian goals is that they may lead to system breakdown (Nuita 1971: 28), which is very often precisely what they intend to accomplish.

I do not for a minute believe that Japan is an idyllic society, nor do I think it likely that it will ever be perfected. Most Japanese take quite the same view, but I would suggest that in this world a considerable advantage accrues to a people who constantly assess their shortcomings and deeply believe that at the very least life could be better, if not for one's self, then for one's children. The world—society—can be a better place, they seem to be saying, if we all each strive to do our best, dedicate ourselves to the full development of our abilities, and contribute to the overall enterprise that small part of it for which we bear direct responsibility. Society can be made better only if all its members do what they must.[26]

In one respect, Japanese this-worldliness imposes on the individual an overwhelming burden. The character of that burden can best be illustrated by an example. When they go to the domestic altar to seek the assistance of the spirits of their forebears in the pursuit of a goal—as many people still do today[27]—the Japanese are in effect asking less for divine intervention in their affairs than a continuation of the unconditional love and support the ancestors gave them while they were yet alive. The burden lies in this: Should they attain their goal, people will offer heartfelt thanks, acknowledging the indispensable contribution of the ancestors to the success of their efforts. Should they fail, however, they will with equal depth of feeling apologize to the ancestral spirits for their shortcomings. Neither the gods nor the ancestors may be blamed for human failure, which is seen to stem rather from some flaw in the person or some insufficiency of effort or dedication on the person's part. At the most mundane level, parents routinely chide their children for making excuses for failure by attempting to shift the blame on others. The unambiguous message is that whatever people accomplish in life ultimately is attributable to the extent to which they have labored to develop their capacities to the fullest. They may obtain support from the groups to which they are admitted, of course, but when all is said and done, the individual alone is responsible. In the end, then, the Japanese view comes down to this: Only through dedication and application can humankind hope to produce in this world the only society and the only fate it will ever know, for there are no others.

Epilogue

Almost exactly 113 years before I delivered the lectures on which this book is based, another Smith brought Lewis Henry Morgan into direct contact with the Japanese. One of the outcomes of that encounter characterizes all subsequent analyses of Japanese society, save the most doctrinaire, for Morgan collected from his informant some ethnographic information that puzzled him. He comments approvingly on evidence that seemed to show that in their upward progress toward civilization, the Japanese "have extricated themselves from the worst evils of barbarism." They make, he notes, a distinction between family and personal names, the point being that "The family name arises after the dawn of civilization." In some other respects, however, his judgment is more harsh: "The political or class divisions of the people are more difficult to be understood. They have, in vigorous development, those cunningly devised gradations of rank which spring up in the transition period from barbarism to civilization, and which the privileged classes are certain to perpetuate long after the absurdity as well as the criminal injustice of legalized rank is perfectly understood in all classes."[1]

What struck him most forcibly, however, was an unexpected discovery with regard to their kinship terminology. "Their system is classific," he wrote. "It is an interesting form for the reason especially that it has passed under the powerful influences arising from the possession of fixed property, and the establishment of laws for its transmission by inheritance. Property rights alone [do not][2] appear to possess sufficient power to overthrow the classificatory system." Further, it seemed to Morgan that the Japanese system must originally have been of the Malayan type, was now apparently passing through the Turanian, and moving clearly in the direction of the Aryan. Because of this peculiar circumstance, he felt obliged to categorize it as Turanian on a purely provisional basis (1871: 431).

After all these years, most assignments of Japan to one analytic category or another remain highly provisional. It may be that the analyst's uncertainty stems from having to show how Japan is unfamiliar by resorting to a vocabulary of the familiar that provides a less than perfect fit. The apparent paradox is that this society, so unlike our own, seems to be able to do almost anything that we do, and sometimes do it better than we have done. No analyst is ever very far removed from the biases of experience and understanding of his or her own society, which color in fundamental ways that analyst's interpretation of other systems. Western observers, clearly made uneasy and insecure by Japanese successes, seek to explain them—or to explain them away. The possibilities seem to most of them to be two in number. Japan today is either just another of several societies like our own, the product of the postindustrial development that characterizes the major powers, or it is a society that well before its modern history began had already developed all the prerequisites for making the transition into industrial modernity on very much the same bases we employed.

The third and far more daunting possibility is the one I have attempted to advance here. It is just conceivable that a society which challenges us in our most cherished certitude of organizational and technological superiority has arrived at its present position by another route, acting on different premises, and proceeding in a direction we have not taken. Surely that is why we seek to reassure ourselves by denying the implications of what we see, for otherwise we should be forced to concede that a system different from our own, without becoming like us, has achieved goals we have long taken to be uniquely ours.

Notes

Introduction

1. See Dole (1960), R. J. Smith (1962a), and Norbeck (1963).
2. See R. J. Smith (1962b).
3. Norbeck (1963: 211) has suggested that were Kawabe really a member of the warrior class, he would almost certainly have taken pains to conceal the fact. Given the extremely low repute in which the Japanese of the period held entertainers, it could only have disgraced him and his family to associate with this "troupe of adventurers" in any capacity.
4. Said (1978: 45) asks, "Can one divide human reality, as human reality seems to be genuinely divided, into clearly different cultures, histories, traditions, societies, even races, and survive the consequences humanly?" The answer must be that to fail to do so is to deny the humanity of others as well as one's own.
5. Even if we make allowances for the fact that they wrote the following passage during the year after the attack on Pearl Harbor, Gregory Bateson and Margaret Mead (1942: 263) render an extraordinarily severe judgment of the Japanese attitude toward their culture and their history: "How the Balinese behaved when the island was invaded by the Japanese we do not yet know—probably having had a pleasant experience of dominion by one power, the Balinese were not overfrightened by the substitution of another. But the Dutch have a record of self-restraint and respect for native customs; the Japanese are notorious exploiters of the helpless, and that firm but passive streak of uncompliance in Balinese character may well invoke savagery from Japanese invaders. The history of culture contact in Japan through the ages has not been happy, and the Japanese, lacking respect for their own culture, perceive their

inevitable inferiority and feel insulted when they meet this self-respect in others." The monograph was published on December 7, 1942, and the section quoted is signed M.M., G.B.

1. THE CREATION OF TRADITION

1. This was the reply when Baelz asked a question about the history of Japan, in which he was much interested (1932: 17).
2. Hirai (1979) offers the only English-language assessment known to me of Green's importance in the exegetical literature on the rescript. See especially her account of the (unacknowledged) borrowing from Green's philosophy by Yoshida Seichi, a major figure in educational policy-making circles, and how Green's views were "Japanized" in the ethics and morals curriculum of the primary and middle schools up to about 1910 (1979:116–22).
3. See Varley (1980: 17–18, 100–1, 119–20) and Kiley (1975). The latter is cited with the author's permission. I have used the list of emperors given in Nelson (1974: 1018–22).
4. Among the most useful treatments of the imperial institution in the Tokugawa and post-Restoration periods are Earl (1964), J. W. Hall (1968), and Webb (1965; 1968).
5. There is a huge and growing literature on the Tokugawa ideologues in general and the Mito scholars in particular. I have found the following particularly useful: Earl (1964), Harootunian (1970), Koschmann (1980), Maruyama (1974), and Najita (1980).
6. Y. Noda (1976) is a good introduction to some of the complexities of the attitudes and values underlying and shaping the modern Japanese legal system.
7. The official English-language text of the constitution is widely available. It appears in Appendixes IX and X of Beckmann (1957: 150–6), which is still a valuable if brief discussion of some of the influences that went into its writing. Siemes (1968: 49–241) gives the full text with the extensive commentaries on it written by the German jurist Hermann Roesler who, as I point out below, played a key role in the making of the constitution.
8. The two indispensable books on *kokutai*, its place in the ethics and morals curriculum, and the popularizations of the concept are by R. K. Hall (1949a; 1949b).
9. Appendix D (1964: 236–9) of this book consists of a highly

compressed account of the historical changes in the meanings and usages of the term.

10. Representative examples of this point of view are Halliday (1975) and Dower's (1975: 3–101) long introduction to the writings of the Canadian historian E. H. Norman.

11. Quoted in Dickins and Lane-Poole (1894: II, 97–8).

12. The only detailed study in English of the sankin-kōtai system, by whose terms the domain lords were required to spend alternate periods of residence in their capitals and in that of the shogun at Edo, now Tokyo, is Tsukahira (1966).

13. For a short account of Roesler's thought and career, as well as an estimate of the extent of his involvement in the drafting of the constitution, see Siemes (1968: 3–46).

14. From the Introduction by Robert Sakai (Haraguchi et al. 1975: 41).

15. A somewhat more detailed discussion of this period and the attempt to construct a national religion can be found in R. J. Smith (1974: 26–30). The many sources cited there deal with various aspects of the complicated situation.

16. Mahayana Buddhism is egalitarian at least in theory in its teaching that in all humans is the potential for buddhahood. See also Weller (1981:58–62). In the Shinto context, Koschmann (1980: 82) notes that Aizawa makes the same point about the effect on witnesses of the First Festival (Daijōsai) celebrated by the emperor: "The conviction of consanguinity injects a strong note of egalitarianism; despite differences in social station, all are minimally authenticated by the divine lineage."

17. Yamamoto (1976: 72) offers the unequivocal view that the Japanese people did regard the emperor as divine, and that some do still: "If there is any Japanese who imitates Americans and feigns surprise at the concept of the 'deified' Tenno [emperor], I would say he is only betraying himself as an ingratiating hypocrite."

18. This extraordinary man's remarkable book rewards careful reading. A German Jew who taught economics in Japan, Singer arrived there when he was forty-five years old. The manuscript was written after the end of World War II and before 1957, while he was teaching at the University of Sydney. He returned to Europe in that year and died in Athens in 1962 at the age

of seventy-six. See the perceptive Introduction by Richard Storry (Singer 1973: 9–21).

19. Gluck (1978) provides a convenient summary of the recent trend in Japanese historiography called *minshūshi,* "people's history." The energies of these scholars are devoted to writing history from the bottom up, which places them squarely in opposition to the Marxist academic establishment in Japan. However deeply concerned with the proletariat, the Marxists find nothing of utility in *la petite histoire* of the common people, apparently. Gluck (1978: 27) makes the point that this new breed of historian is largely made up of men now for the most part in their fifties, which has led them to take a particular interest in that period of their own lives that I have just discussed—the years during which the values of the "emperor system" were being made orthodox.

20. See Najita's (1980: 127–37) discussion of "twentieth-century restorationism."

21. Although there is a vast Japanese-language archive of published and unpublished material from this period, as well as innumerable retrospective accounts of the popular reaction to the imperial orthodoxy of the 1930s, there is little material from that time in English. One of the few detailed contemporary English-language sources is R. J. Smith and Wiswell (1982).

2 ORDER AND DIFFUSENESS

1. For discussions of the *kokugakusha,* see Harootunian (1970), Najita (1980: 55–9), Matsumoto (1970). For a recent discussion of the importance of Confucianism in the formation of the Japanese world view, see Morishima (1982).

2. Eleanor Westney, personal communication, provided the figures on Edo. Befu (1965) is one of the clearest statements on the issue of village autonomy.

3. Quoted by Kawashima (1968: 431).

4. Quoted by Maruyama (1974: 170).

5. The former Beatle's initial intransigence and protestations of ignorance soon altered to making an admission of fault. This saved him from being imprisoned, and he was deported after being detained for several days. A very similar view obtains in China. Jiang Qing, widow of Mao Zedong, enraged the court by her refusal to admit her guilt during the show trial of the Gang

of Four in the winter of 1980. She was found guilty, of course, and the assumption is that the penalty imposed upon her was all the harsher for her stubborn refusal to admit to the crimes of which she was charged.

6. Y. Noda (1976: xii) reports that there were 1,748,344 court cases in 1964 and 1,752,150 in 1973. The per capita rate is thus declining, and he attributes the misperception that it has risen to the increase in publicity given several major suits in recent years. He also notes (1976: 182) that cases that come to the courts with great frequency involve large corporations which are in competition in purely economic terms and suits involving lender and borrower.

7. Reporting on a study of a town in Georgia, Greenhouse (1981: 13) comments on the reasons for the total avoidance of the courts by the Southern Baptists of the community: "The ideology proscribes litigation and, in fact, any attempts at redress apart from unilateral forgiveness or prayer. They cite the New Testament: Romans 13: 18–19 exhorts Christians to 'avenge not yourselves . . . : for it is written vengeance is mine, I will repay, saith the Lord.' The town's Baptists interpret this passage as prohibiting remedial initiatives involving any third party but Jesus. To do otherwise is sacrilege, a failure of faith." The court itself is viewed as a profane institution.

8. Nader (1978: 95) probably would not go so far, but in the following passage offers a similar caution: "A nation such as the United States which is dominated by contract relationships and which also pays less attention to the ethical implications of cases, is developing a law that is predominantly mechanical and that may be moving in the direction of a law that is no longer pertinent to the needs of the many." In his second article on Japan's law, Haley (1982: 281) seems to have undergone a change of heart. He concludes his discussion of the relative advantages and disadvantages of what he calls "sanctionless law" with the following observation: "To strengthen legal sanctions to make the courts more efficient and judicial remedies more effective, or by any means to broaden the enforcement of law through the legal process, would inevitably corrode the social structure that now exists."

9. See the Introduction by Robert Sakai (Haraguchi et al. 1975: 15).

10. Nakamura (1964: 362). Suzuki (1978: 139) is quite wrong in suggesting that persons "play fixed roles, which should not vary even with a change in time or place."

11. Fruin (1980) offers a stimulating discussion of the relationship between the stem-family model (the household) and the organization of a major Japanese firm.

12. For a set of detailed case studies of Quality Control circles in action, see Asian Productivity Organization (1972).

13. Pascale (1978) emphasizes the use of ambiguity as a managerial tool.

14. Atsumi (1979) is the only English-language source that discusses in any detail the importance of after-work association by co-workers in Japan.

15. Although the context is neither democratic nor egalitarian, it is by no means as grimly authoritarian or exploitative as the American might expect it to be, for "although both American and Japanese employers try to reconcile individual and organizational goals, the Japanese tend to focus on adapting organizational principles to employee needs . . . as long as [the adaptation] does not endanger high level management goals" (Cole 1979: 242). John W. Hall (1974: 48) has pointed out that Confucian ideology supports a rigid status hierarchy, but equally imposes upon those in positions of authority the requirement that they exercise it with humaneness. Thus what he calls "rule by status" in the Tokugawa period was rendered acceptable by combining ideological support for authority with the injunction that those who govern be responsible and benevolent.

16. For discussions of permanent employment and lifetime commitment, see Cole (1979: 11–25) and Dore (1973: 31–41).

17. He also observes that no manager extols the virtues of dependence, but rather attempts to promote a sense of interdependence by focusing on the values of cooperation, teamwork, and mutual support, while denigrating self-centeredness and the pursuit of self-interest (Cole 1979: 249). For a very different view of the relationship of the assembly-line worker to the company, see Junkerman (1982) on the Nissan Motor Plant at Zama. He argues that the company and its union have united to mass-produce cooperative and efficient workers just as effectively as the assembly line produces Datsun subcompacts.

Charging both with the widespread use of "control and intimi-
dation," Junkerman appears to assume that such practices are
alien, for example, to UAW locals and American management
at the plant level. He also seems to think that workers cannot
be made cooperative and productive save by coercion. Kamata
(1982) has given us a more extended account of the lot of
a temporary worker at a Toyota plant in 1972–3. Ronald
Dore's introduction provides the indispensable historical and
social contexts of Kamata's polemic.

3 SELF AND OTHER

1. Yet at the end he confesses he finds the Japanese solution
   profoundly appealing and admits that were he to be exiled from
   Europe, he would choose Japan over any other country in which
   to live (Koestler 1961: 274–5).

2. DeVos (1973) contains eighteen papers by him and his col-
   laborators Wagatsuma Hiroshi, Mizushima Keiichi, and the late
   William Caudill.

3. Miller (1967: 32) provides a list of historically attested forms
   for speaker and person spoken to which, while it does not aim
   at exhaustiveness, is nonetheless of formidable length.

4. Wolff (1980) presents a very useful analysis of the sociolin-
   guistic literature on personal referents in Japanese, from which
   I have taken much of the material that follows in the text.

5. In addition to the two phonetic syllabaries in common use,
   written Japanese employs a very large number of Chinese
   characters. A given character has from one to a half-dozen or
   more standard readings or pronunciations, which are to be
   found in any good dictionary along with the meaning or
   meanings of the character. It is in personal names and to a
   large extent in place names as well that the Japanese have
   pushed variant readings of the characters to extraordinary
   lengths. There are dictionaries devoted in their entirety to
   setting forth all the attested readings of the characters that
   have been used in names, but in any directory or bibliography
   one will find a significant number of names at whose pronunciation one can only guess. Even if the name dictionary offers
   a number of variant readings, it is not possible to determine
   which of them is used by the person one wishes to look up,

for something approaching free variation in choice of reading exists.

6. Nakano Takashi, personal communication, 1972.

7. Actually there is a striking exception to this generalization. Alone among the Japanese the emperor uses the first-person referent *chin*. In the West, the best we can do is the royal "We."

8. The exact opposite is more likely the case, according to Miller (1971: 662), who argues that all the evidence shows that the system of *keigo* is becoming increasingly complex.

9. The Japanese did adopt the Chinese titles of Great Minister of the Left (*sadaijin*) and Great Minister of the Right (*udaijin*) at an early period and assigned them precedence in that order. The Russian ship's captain Golownin (1824: I, 140) noted that during his captivity in Japan, when he and members of his crew were lined up for interrogation, he was invariably seated at the left with the others to his right in descending order of rank: "The Japanese reckon the left side superior to the right. We remarked their attention to this, in all cases, and were informed by themselves, that they considered that side the post of distinction; they could assign no reason for the preference." In more recent times the distinction is made between the political parties of the left and right, a clear borrowing from the West, and lefthandedness used to be "corrected" in school as an aberrant condition. There are, however, no equations of left and right with other binary pairs such as defilement and purity, illegitimate and legitimate, black and white, and so on. And although the word left (*hidari*) occurs in expressions having to do with perversity or oddity, decline of fortune, and drinking (not necessarily defined as an evil habit), it is also an element in the expression *hidari-uchiwa* (a fan in the left hand), meaning to live a life of ease.

10. Quoted in Miyoshi (1979: 88–9).

11. See R. J. Smith (1974: 82–4) for a discussion of the names on memorial tablets.

12. I must apologize to Koji Taira for the disappointment he is bound to feel in the use I have made of his generous review of my book in which I discuss a conflict that arose within a small community (R. J. Smith 1978: 229–48). He took my account to mean that I had exploded the myth of consensual and har-

148 *Japanese society*

monious Japan, but did not see that I was equally at pains to show how attempts were being made to heal the rupture and restore relations insofar as possible. See Taira (1979).

13. The untouchables are the subject of most of the papers in DeVos and Wagatsuma (1966). For a vigorous Marxian dissent from both the popular and the official Japanese views of the recent history of these people, see Ruyle (1979). Hane (1982) offers an extended treatment of other disadvantaged groups in Japanese society.

14. See pages 68–9.

15. The theatrical nature of Mishima's act was heightened by the fact that it was prefigured in his well-known short story Yūkoku (Patriotism), subsequently made into a notorious film in which Mishima himself played the role of the ill-starred military officer who commits seppuku in the wake of the failed coup d'état of February 26, 1936 (Mishima 1966). Both story and film are excruciating examples of "patriotic gore."

16. Yet it will not do to let the charge against the Japanese pass without some comment on the issue of the rarity of purely principled behavior in the West as well. "When a man lives up to his principles we are all amazed, and count it a virtue whatever the principles; and our amazement is as rare as the occurrence, so that neither is called upon often" (Feibelman 1956: 368).

17. In his study of three generations of Japanese Americans, Connor (1977: 107–9) found that few of the third-generation (sansei) respondents were able to identify words belonging to the rich vocabulary of obligations—on, giri, gimu, chū, ninjō— with which their parents and grandparents had grown up. But 17 percent of the males and 23 percent of the females knew the meaning of gaman, while enryo (see pages 83–4) was identified correctly by 25 percent of the males and 36 percent of the females.

18. Frager and Rohlen (1976) is the best single source in English on seishin training and philosophy. I have made liberal use of their discussion in the paragraphs that follow.

19. He later wrote a book that sold nearly one million copies and subsequently was elected to the national Diet, where he served for six years. One account (Mainichi Daily News

1975: 342) refers to his use of "hard training coupled with spiritualism."
20. Quoted in Rustin (1976: 72).

4. The perfectible society

1. Quoted in Allen and Donnithorne (1954: 225).
2. Quoted in the *Asahi Evening News* (Tokyo), March 30, 1979.
3. The cartoon is *Fuji Santarō*, drawn by Satō Sanpei, and appeared in the *Asahi Shinbun* (Tokyo) of April 7, 1979. The lyrics, a parody of the ditty (here called *EC ondo*), are: *EC no keizai san, naze nihon kirau? Hirune, hiruzake, yasumu koto ga dai suki de, so-o-re de nihon kirau. Katte da na! Katte da na!*
4. I am indebted to Stephen Nussbaum for calling my attention to Yanagita Kunio's (1969: 205) suggestion that there are certain affinities between the word *mukashi* ("long ago," often used in folktales to begin a story and usually translated, "Once upon a time" in that context) and *mukō* ("over there" or "the far side").
5. Pelzel (1970a) is the source for the discussion of the myths that follows. His view of the Japanese as essentially optimistic is flatly contradicted by Morris (1973: 39), who finds them profoundly pessimistic in their orientation to the world and human endeavor.
6. One of these that has been translated is Ishida (1974). Suzuki (1978) is in the same genre, although he is more directly concerned with the Japanese language. By far the most entertaining and astringent examples of this impatient reaction are those by Miller; see his discussion of studies of the Japanese language (1977). More general essays on the topic will be found in Mouer and Sugimoto (1980).
7. Quoted in Earl (1964: 214).
8. Miyoshi (1979: 124), citing Maruyama Masao.
9. William B. Hauser reminds me that in the late Tokugawa period, while some of the ideologues were expressing such sentiments, highly pragmatic and adaptive responses to problems of production in agriculture and many other activities were routinely being experimented with, particularly in the form of technological innovation. Harootunian (1966) discusses the increasing emphasis in Tokugawa Confucianism on what was called

"practical learning" (*jitsugaku*) at the expense of the development of the more abstruse element of neo–Confucianism.

10. I have taken the text from Lu (1974: II, 176–7) and edited it slightly. The resonances with the past are quite direct, for the memorable phrase "enduring the unendurable and suffering what is insufferable" is taken from the Meiji emperor's rescript issued at the time of the Triple Intervention (Shillony 1981: 87), when Russia, Germany, and France forced Japan to abandon its claim to the Liaotung Peninsula following its victory in the Sino-Japanese War of 1894–5.

11. For a discussion of the Confucian conception of the nature of man as good or evil, see Ching (1977: 72–4) and Yearley (1980: 465).

12. See the concluding chapter, "Can We Learn from the Japanese?" in Cole (1979: 251–63).

13. Takezawa and Whitehill (1981) report that in 1975, 73 percent of the Japanese workers they interviewed said they felt their company to be more important, or at least as important as their private life, representing an increase over their findings in 1968. This trend was observed among young and older workers alike.

14. Cited in Ike (1978: 113).

15. Tada (1978) provides the most balanced treatment of the phenomenon of my-home-ism in English.

16. Roden (1980) has given us an invaluable account of the First Higher School (*Ichikō*) in Tokyo and the often brutal socialization by their peers of the young men who attended it. There are few English-language studies of the once widespread age-grade societies at the village level. One is Johnson (1975), which is remarkable for its firsthand observation and partial participation in a peer group of adolescent males in a village not far from Tokyo. Such groups, called *shōnendan*, were still very common in the interwar years of which Singer wrote.

17. That such perfectibility of human nature is attainable is reflected in management's policies and strategies directed toward workers, especially male employees of large-scale firms (Cole 1979: 222–3). The search for perfection is also institutionalized in the form of *hansei kai* (self-criticism meetings), held after events and performances organized and staged by school and other community groups. In these meetings, the inadequacies of plan-

ning and execution are discussed openly, and because they are
routine, appear to be acceptable vehicles for directing critical
comments at individuals as well as reviewing overall shortcomings. They invariably conclude with a consensual commitment
to do better next time. The *hansei kai*, far from being a relic
of the past, flourishes in new suburban community associations
today (Stephen Nussbaum: personal communication, 1980).

18. Here I take issue with Kracht (1980: 344), who maintains that
"on the basis of our previous knowledge we may articulate the
hypothesis that the non-existence of a creator-deity as central to
the definition of religious consciousness does not, even given the
permanent secularization of thought, suggest the postulation
of a concept analogous to that of the modern Western idea
of man as 'creator' of his own world." I share Chan's view that
we must in fact advance that very postulate (1978: 174).

19. There are a number of useful sources on crime control and the
criminal justice system in contemporary Japan. Among them are
Bayley (1976), Clifford (1976), Ames (1981), and the Citizens'
Crime Commission of Philadelphia (1975). Bayley and Ames
are particularly valuable in that both report on the behavior of
police officers "on the beat."

20. The "people's historians" referred to earlier take violent exception to Nakane's conclusion that there can be no revolution
in this vertical society (Gluck 1978: 37).

21. I am grateful to Jonathan H. Wolff for sharing with me the
results of his research on the origins of the Narita imbroglio.

22. The classic work in English is Borton (1968), a reprint of the
original 1938 study with a new introduction by the author; see
also Burton (1979).

23. William B. Hauser, personal communication.

24. McKean (1981) provides a useful discussion of the varieties of
these "citizens' movements" and the extent to which they limit
their objectives to influencing local government, a tactic she
suggests is born of the highly pragmatic view that to aim at
higher governmental levels would be fruitless.

25. As Durkheim (1933: 13) remarked: "Now the subordination
of private utility to common utility, whatever it may be, always
has a moral character, for it necessarily implies sacrifice and
abnegation."

26. The conservatively cautious nature of this orientation is reflected

in the 1978 Survey of National Character in responses to the question, "Of the following ways of thinking about society, which is closest to your point of view?" Three percent thought that "The structure of society today should be changed overnight by revolution"; 4 percent opted for "The social system must be maintained at any cost"; 89 percent felt that "The bad points of society should be reformed gradually" (Prime Minister's Statistical Office 1979: 193).

27. Many foreigners seem to doubt that this must be the case, and for reasons that are not entirely clear to me, many Japanese steadfastly deny that they repair to the ancestors in time of trouble. "A few years ago, after presenting some of my materials on ancestor worship in Japan to a group of [American] students, I was challenged by a young man who angrily denied the possibility that members of a capitalist industrial society could, as he put it, still be praying to the spirits of their ancestors. My claim to the contrary struck him as perverse, for it made no sense to him because of what he saw as an obvious incongruity, an incompatibility between practice and context. I realized finally that *his* position arose from his assumption that the Japanese are exactly what he mistakenly thought Americans are like, but the point is that he saw a contradiction and I did not" (R. J. Smith 1977: 6). Subsequently, at an international conference on ancestors, the late Takeda Chōshu broadened the point considerably. When someone asked why ancestor worship persists in modern Japan, he said: "That is not an interesting question. The real question is why it died out in the West."

Epilogue

1. Morgan (1871: 425–31) discusses "The Japanese Nation" at some length. I have taken all the quoted passages from this section of his monograph.
2. I have inserted the words "do not" here because the sentence seems to me to make no sense as it stands (Morgan 1871: 430).

Bibliography

Allen, G. C. and Audrey G. Donnithorne
1954   Western Enterprise in Far Eastern Economic Development:
China and Japan. London: George Allen and Unwin.
Ames, Walter L.
1981   Police and Community in Japan. Berkeley and Los Angeles:
University of California Press.
Anonymous
1978   "Narita: trouble-ridden airport" Japan Quarterly 25, 3:
251–5.
Anonymous
1981   "Mini-management course" NetWorking: A Newsletter by
Employees . . . For Employees (Cornell University) 2,2: 2.
Anonymous
1982   "A lawyer by any other name . . ." Journal of Japanese Trade
and Industry 6: 58–9.
Asian Productivity Organization
1972   Japan Quality Control Circles: Quality Control Circle Case
Studies. Tokyo: Asian Productivity Organization.
Atsumi, Reiko
1979   "Tsukiai—obligatory personal relationships of Japanese
white-collar company employees" Human Organization 38,
1: 63–70.
Azumi, Koya and Charles J. McMillan
1976   "Worker sentiment in the Japanese factory: its organizational determinants" In Lewis Austin, editor, Japan: The
Paradox of Progress. New Haven, Conn.: Yale University
Press. Pp. 215–30.

Baelz, Erwin (edited by Toku Baelz)
1932 Awakening Japan: The Diary of a German Doctor. New York: Viking Press.
Barnlund, Dean C.
1975 Public and Private Self in Japan and the United States: Communicative Styles of Two Cultures: Tokyo: Simul Press.
Bateson, Gregory and Margaret Mead
1942 Balinese Character: A Photographic Analysis. New York: Special Publications of the New York Academy of Sciences, Volume II.
Bayley, David H.
1976 Forces of Order: Police Behavior in Japan and the United States. Berkeley and Los Angeles: University of California Press.
Beasley, W. G.
1972 The Meiji Restoration. Stanford, Calif.: Stanford University Press.
Beckmann, George M.
1957 The Making of the Meiji Constitution: The Oligarchs and the Constitutional Development of Japan, 1868–1891. Lawrence: University of Kansas Press.
Befu, Harumi
1962 "Corporate emphasis and patterns of descent in the Japanese family" In Robert J. Smith and Richard K. Beardsley, editors, Japanese Culture: Its Development and Characteristics. Chicago: Aldine. Pp. 34–41.
1965 "Village autonomy and articulation with the state: the case of Tokugawa Japan" Journal of Asian Studies 25, 1: 19–32.
Bell, Ronald (editor)
1973 The Japanese Experience. Tokyo: Weatherhill.
Bellah, Robert N.
1957 Tokugawa Religion: The Values of Pre-Industrial Japan. Glencoe, Ill.: Free Press.
Berger, Peter L. and Thomas Luckmann
1966 The Social Construction of Reality. Garden City, N.Y.: Doubleday.
Bikle, George B., Jr.
1971 "Utopia and the planning element in modern Japan" In

David W. Plath, editor, Aware of Utopia. Urbana: University of Illinois Press. Pp. 33–54.

Black, John R.
1883   Young Japan: Yokohama and Edo. New York: Baker, Pratt. Two volumes.

Borton, Hugh
1968   Peasant Uprisings in Japan of the Tokugawa Period. New York: Paragon Book Gallery. 2nd edition.

Bowring, Richard J.
1979   Mori Ogai and the Modernization of Japanese Culture. Cambridge, Eng.: Cambridge University Press.

Burton, W. Donald
1979   "Peasant movements in early Tokugawa Japan" Peasant Studies 8, 3: 59–73.

Caiger, John
1968   "The aims and content of school courses in Japanese history, 1872–1945" In Edmund Skrzypczak, editor, Japan's Modern Century. Tokyo: Sophia University. Pp. 51–81.

Caudill, William
1972   "Tiny dramas: vocal communication between mother and infant in Japanese and American families" In William P. Lebra, editor, Transcultural Research in Mental Health. Honolulu: The University Press of Hawaii. Pp. 25–48.

Chan, Wing-tsit
1978   "Review of Julia Ching Confucianism and Christianity: A Comparative Study" Journal of Asian Studies 38, 1: 173–5.

Chang, Hao
1980   "Neo–Confucian moral thought and its modern legacy" Journal of Asian Studies 39, 2: 259–72.

Ching, Julia
1977   Confucianism and Christianity: A Comparative Study. Tokyo: Kodansha International.

Citizens Crime Commission of Philadelphia
1975   Tokyo: One City Where Crime Doesn't Pay! Philadelphia: Citizens Crime Commission of Philadelphia.

Clark, Rodney
1979   The Japanese Company. New Haven, Conn.: Yale University Press.

Clifford, William
  1976 Crime Control in Japan. Lexington, Mass.: D. C. Heath.
Cole, Robert E.
  1971 Japanese Blue Collar: The Changing Tradition. Berkeley and
         Los Angeles: University of California Press.
  1976 "Changing labor-force characteristics and their impact on
         Japanese industrial relations" In Lewis Austin, editor, Japan:
         The Paradox of Progress. New Haven, Conn.: Yale Univer-
         sity Press. Pp. 165–213.
  1979 Work, Mobility, and Participation: A Comparative Study
         of American and Japanese Industry. Berkeley and Los
         Angeles: University of California Press.
Connor, John W.
  1977 Tradition and Change in Three Generations of Japanese
         Americans. Chicago: Nelson-Hall.
Cummings, William K.
  1980 Education and Equality in Japan. Princeton, N.J.: Prince-
         ton University Press.
DeVos, George A.
  1973 Socialization for Achievement: Essays on the Cultural
         Psychology of the Japanese. Berkeley and Los Angeles:
         University of California Press.
DeVos, George A. and Hiroshi Wagatsuma (editors)
  1966 Japan's Invisible Race. Caste in Culture and Personality.
         Berkeley and Los Angeles: University of California Press.
Dickins, Frederick V. and Stanley Lane-Poole
  1894 The Life of Sir Harry Parkes. London: Macmillan. Two
         volumes.
Doi, Takeo (translated by John Bester)
  1973 The Anatomy of Dependence (Amae no kōzō). Tokyo:
         Kodansha International.
Dole, Gertrude E.
  1960 "The classification of Yankee nomenclature in the light
         of the evolution of kinship" In Gertrude E. Dole and
         Robert L. Carneiro, editors, Essays in the Science of Cul-
         ture. New York: Thomas Y. Crowell. Pp. 162–78.
Dore, Ronald P.
  1958 City Life in Japan: A Study of a Tokyo Ward. Berkeley
         and Los Angeles: University of California Press.
  1964 "Education: Japan" In Robert E. Ward and Dankwart A.
         Rustow, editors, Political Modernization in Japan and

Turkey. Princeton, N.J.: Princeton University Press. Pp. 176–204.
1973   British Factory, Japanese Factory: The Origins of National Diversity in Industrial Relations. Berkeley and Los Angeles: University of California Press.
Dower, John W.
1975   "E. H. Norman, Japan and the uses of history" In John W. Dower, editor, Origins of the Modern Japanese State: Selected Writings of E. H. Norman. New York: Pantheon. Pp. 3–101.
Durkheim, Emile
1933   The Division of Labor in Society. New York: Macmillan.
Earl, David M.
1964   Emperor and Nation in Japan: Political Thinkers of the Tokugawa Period. Seattle: University of Washington Press.
Evans, Robert Jr.
1977   "Changing labor markets and criminal behavior in Japan" Journal of Asian Studies 36, 3: 477–89.
Feibelman, James K.
1956   The Institutions of Society. London: Allen and Unwin.
Frager, Robert and Thomas P. Rohlen
1976   "The future of tradition: Japanese spirit in the 1980s" In Lewis Austin, editor, Japan: The Paradox of Progress. New Haven, Conn.: Yale University Press. Pp. 255–78.
Fruin, W. Mark
1980   "The family as a firm and the firm as a family in Japan: the case of Kikkoman Shōyu Company Limited" Journal of Family History 5, 4: 432–49.
Furukawa, Tesshi
1968   "The individual in Japanese ethics" In Charles A. Moore, editor, The Status of the Individual in East and West. Honolulu: University of Hawaii Press. Pp. 301–27.
Gates, Hill
1979   "Dependency and the part-time proletariat in Taiwan" Modern China 5, 3: 381–408.
Gluck, Carol
1978   "The people in history: recent trends in Japanese historiography" Journal of Asian Studies 38, 1: 25–50.
Golownin, V. M.
1824   Memoirs of a Captivity in Japan, During the Years 1811,

1812, and 1813. London: Henry Colburn. Three volumes.

Greenhouse, Carol J.
1981   "Nature is to culture as suing is to praying: legal pluralism in an American suburb" Mimeographed, 34 pages.

Haley, John Owen
1978   "The myth of the reluctant litigant" Journal of Japanese Studies 4, 2: 359–90.
1982   "Sheathing the sword of justice in Japan: an essay on law without sanctions" Journal of Japanese Studies 8, 2: 265–81.

Hall, John W.
1968   "A monarch for modern Japan" In Robert E. Ward, editor, Political Development in Modern Japan. Princeton, N.J.: Princeton University Press. Pp. 11–64.
1974   "Rule by status in Tokugawa Japan" Journal of Japanese Studies 1, 1: 39–49.

Hall, Robert King
1949a Kokutai no Hongi: Cardinal Principles of the National Entity of Japan (translated by John Owen Gauntlett). Cambridge, Mass.: Harvard University Press.
1949b Shushin: The Ethics of a Defeated Nation. New York: Bureau of Publications, Columbia Teachers College, Columbia University.

Halliday, Jon
1975   A Political History of Japanese Capitalism. New York: Pantheon.

Hane, Mikiso
1982   Peasants, Rebels, and Outcasts: The Underside of Modern Japan. New York: Pantheon.

Haraguchi, Torao, Robert K. Sakai, Mitsugu Sakihara, Kazuko Yamada, and Masato Matsui
1975   The Status System and Social Organization of Satsuma: A Translation of the Shumon Tefuda Aratame Jomoku. Honolulu: University Press of Hawaii.

Harootunian, Harry D.
1966   "Jinsei, jinzai, and jitsugaku: social values and leadership in late Tokugawa thought" In Bernard S. Silberman and Harry D. Harootunian, editors, Modern Japanese Leadership: Transition and Change. Tucson: University of Arizona Press. Pp. 82–119.

1970   Toward Restoration. Berkeley and Los Angeles: University of California Press.
Hayashi, Chikio
1975   "Time, age and ways of thinking from the *Kokuminsei* surveys" In David W. Plath, editor, Adult Episodes in Japan. Journal of Asian and African Studies (Special Number) 10, 1–2: 75–85.
1976   "Changes in Japanese thought during the past twenty years" In Text of Seminar on Changing Values in Modern Japan. Tokyo: Nihonjin Kenkyukai and the Asia Foundation. Pp. 3–57.
Henderson, Dan Fenno
1965   Conciliation and Japanese Law: Tokugawa and Modern. Seattle: University of Washington Press. Two volumes.
1968   "The evolution of Tokugawa law" In John W. Hall and Marius B. Jansen, editors, Studies in the Institutional History of Modern Japan. Princeton, N.J.: Princeton University Press. Pp. 203–29.
1975   Village "Contracts" in Tokugawa Japan: Fifty Specimens with English Translations and Comments. Seattle: University of Washington Press.
Higa, Masanori
1972   "The use of the imperative mood in postwar Japan" In William P. Lebra, editor, Transcultural Research in Mental Health. Honolulu: University Press of Hawaii. Pp. 49–56.
Hirai, Atsuko
1979   "Self-realization and the common good: T. H. Green in Meiji ethical thought" Journal of Japanese Studies 5, 1: 107–36.
Ike, Nobutaka
1978   A Theory of Japanese Democracy. Boulder, Colo.: Westview Press.
Ishida, Eiichiro (translated by Teruko Kachi)
1974   Japanese Culture: A Study of Origins and Characteristics (*Nihon bunka ron*). Honolulu: University Press of Hawaii.
Jansen, Marius B.
1970   "The Meiji state: 1868–1912" In James B. Crowley, editor, Modern East Asia: Essays in Interpretation. New York: Harcourt, Brace and World. Pp. 95–121.

Junkerman, John
   1982   " 'We Are Driven' ": life on the fast line at Datsun"
          Mother Jones 7, 7: 21–23, 38–40.
Johnson, Thomas W.
   1975   Shonendan: Adolescent Peer Group Socialization in Rural
          Japan. Taipei: Orient Cultural Service.
Kamata, Satoshi (translated by Akimoto Tatsuru)
   1982   Japan in the Passing Lane: An Insider's Account of Life
          in a Japanese Auto Factory. New York: Pantheon.
Kawashima, Takeyoshi
   1963   "Dispute resolution in contemporary Japan" In Arthur
          Taylor von Mehren, editor, Law in Japan: The Legal
          Order in a Changing Society. Cambridge, Mass.: Harvard
          University Press. Pp. 41–72.
   1968   "The status of the individual in the notion of law, right,
          and social order in Japan" In Charles A. Moore, editor,
          The Status of the Individual in East and West. Honolulu:
          University of Hawaii Press. Pp. 429–48.
Kiefer, Christie
   1976   "The *danchi zoku* and the evolution of metropolitan mind"
          In Lewis Austin, editor, Japan: The Paradox of Progress.
          New Haven, Conn.: Yale University Press. Pp. 279–300.
Kiley, Cornelius J.
   1975   "Marriage and succession in the archaic Japanese dynasty"
          Paper read at the Pacific Regional Conference of the Asso-
          ciation for Asian Studies.
Kinmonth, Earl H.
   1981   The Self-Made Man in Meiji Japanese Thought: From
          Samurai to Salary Man. Berkeley and Los Angeles: Univer-
          sity of California Press.
Koestler, Arthur
   1961   The Lotus and the Robot. New York: Macmillan.
Kogane, Yoshihiro
   1975   "Value judgments and economic activities of Japanese
          people: a dynamic economy and a stable culture" In
          Gianni Fodella, editor, Social Structures and Economic
          Dynamics in Japan up to 1980. Milan: Institute of Eco-
          nomic and Social Studies for East Asia, Luigi Bocconi
          University, Series on East Asian Economy and Society.
          Vol. I, pp. 187–98.

Koschmann, J. Victor
  1980 Discourse in Action: Representational Politics in Mito in the
       Late Tokugawa Period. Unpublished PhD dissertation, Uni-
       versity of Chicago.
Kracht, Klaus
  1980 "Review of Japanese Thought in the Tokugawa Period,
       1600–1868: Methods and Metaphors, edited by Tetsuo
       Najita and Irwin Scheiner" Journal of Japanese Studies
       6, 2: 331–53.
Lebra, Takie Sugiyama
  1974 "Intergenerational continuity and discontinuity in moral
       values among the Japanese: a preliminary report" In
       William P. Lebra, editor, Youth, Socialization, and
       Mental Health. Honolulu: University Press of Hawaii.
       Pp. 247–74.
  1976 Japanese Patterns of Behavior. Honolulu: University Press
       of Hawaii.
Lu, David John
  1974 Sources of Japanese History: New York: McGraw Hill.
       Two volumes.
Mainichi Daily News
  1975 Fifty Years of Light and Dark: The Hirohito Era [Edited
       by the staff of the Mainichi Newspapers]. Tokyo: Mainichi
       Newspapers.
Maraini, Fosco
  1975 "Japan and the future: some suggestions from nihonjin-ron
       literature" In Gianni Fodella, editor, Social Structures
       and Economic Dynamics in Japan up 1980. Milan: Insti-
       tute of Economic and Social Studies for East Asia, Luigi
       Bocconi University, Series on East Asian Economy and
       Society. Vol. I, pp. 15–77.
Maruyama, Masao (translated by Mikiso Hane)
  1974 Studies in the Intellectual History of Tokugawa Japan.
       Princeton, N.J.: Princeton University Press.
Matsumoto, Shigeru
  1970 Motoori Norinaga 1730–1801. Cambridge, Mass.: Harvard
       University Press.
McKean, Margaret A.
  1981 Environmental Protest and Citizen Politics in Japan. Berke-
       ley and Los Angeles: University of California Press.

Miller, Roy Andrew
    1967   The Japanese Language. Chicago: University of Chicago
            Press.
    1971   "Levels of speech (*keigo*) and the Japanese linguistic
            response to modernization" In Donald H. Shively, editor,
            Tradition and Modernization in Japanese Culture. Prince-
            ton, N.J.: Princeton University Press. Pp. 601–67.
    1977   The Japanese Language in Contemporary Japan. Washing-
            ton, D.C.: American Enterprise Institute for Public Policy
            Research.
Mishima, Yukio (translated by Geoffrey W. Sargent)
    1966   "Patriotism" [*Yūkoko*]. In Mishima Yukio, Death in
            Midsummer and Other Stories. New York: New Directions.
            Pp. 93–118.
Miyoshi, Masao
    1974   Accomplices of Silence: The Modern Japanese Novel. Berke-
            ley and Los Angeles: University of California Press.
    1979   As We Saw Them: The First Japanese Embassy in the
            United States (1860). Berkeley and Los Angeles: University
            of California Press.
Morgan, Lewis Henry
    1871   Systems of Consanguinity and Affinity of the Human
            Family. Washington, D.C.: Smithsonian Contributions to
            Knowledge, 17, Smithsonian Institution.
Morisaki, Kazue
    1973   "Two languages, two souls" Concerned Theatre in Japan
            2, 3 & 4: 153–65.
Morishima, Michio
    1982   Why Has Japan "Succeeded"? Western Technology and
            the Japanese Ethos. Cambridge University Press.
Morris, Ivan
    1975   The Nobility of Failure: Tragic Heroes in the History of
            Japan. New York: Holt, Rinehart and Winston.
Mouer, Ross and Yoshio Sugimoto
    1980   "Japanese society: reappraisals and new directions" Social
            Analysis 5/6 (Special Issue).
Nader, Laura
    1978   "The direction of law and the development of extra-
            judicial processes in nation state societies" In Peter H.
            Gulliver, editor, Cross-Examinations: Essays in Memory

of Max Gluckman. Leiden: E. J. Brill. Pp. 78–95.

Nagashima, Nobuhiro
1973 "A reversed world: or is it?" In Robin Horton and Ruth Finnegan, editors, Modes of Thought: Essays on Thinking in Western and Non-Western Societies. London: Faber and Faber. Pp. 92–111.

Najita, Tetsuo
1980 Japan: The Intellectual Foundations of Modern Japanese Politics. Chicago: University of Chicago Press.

Najita, Tetsuo and J. Victor Koschmann (editors)
1982 Conflict in Modern Japanese History: The Neglected Tradition. Princeton, N.J.: Princeton University Press.

Nakamura, Hajime
1964 Ways of Thinking of Eastern Peoples: India–China–Tibet–Japan. Honolulu: East-West Center Press.
1968 "Consciousness of the individual and the universal among the Japanese" In Charles A. Moore, editor, The Status of the Individual in East and West. Honolulu: University of Hawaii Press. Pp. 141–60.

Nakane, Chie
1970 Japanese Society. Berkeley and Los Angeles: University of California Press.

Nelson, Andrew N.
1974 The Modern Reader's Japanese-English Character Dictionary. Tokyo: Tuttle. 2nd revised edition.

Noda, Mitz
1980 "The Japanese way" Executive (Graduate School of Business and Public Administration, Cornell University) 6, 3: 22–25.

Noda, Yosiyuki (translated and edited by Anthony H. Angelo)
1976 Introduction to Japanese Law. Tokyo: University of Tokyo Press.

Norbeck, Edward
1963 "Lewis Henry Morgan and Japanese terms of relationship: profit through error" Southwestern Journal of Anthropology 19, 2: 208–15.

Nuita, Seiji
1971 "Traditional utopias in Japan and the West: a study in contrasts" In David W. Plath, editor, Aware of Utopia. Urbana: University of Illinois Press. Pp. 12–32.

Ōkuma, Shigenobu
   1910 "Conclusion" in Okuma Shigenobu, Compiler (edited by Marcus B. Huish) Fifty Years of New Japan. London: Smith, Elder. Two volumes. II: 554–79.
Oliphant, Laurence
   1860 Narrative of the Earl of Elgin's Mission to China and Japan in the Years 1857, '58, '59. New York: Harper.
Omicinski, John
   1981 "Japanese company boosts Auburn's economy" Ithaca Journal (Gannett News Service), April 29.
Pascale, Richard T.
   1978 "Zen and the art of management" Harvard Business Review 56, 2: 153–62.
Pelzel, John C.
   1970a "Human nature in the Japanese myths" In Albert M. Craig and Donald H. Shively, editors, Personality in Japanese History. Berkeley and Los Angeles: University of California Press. Pp. 29–56.
   1970b "Japanese kinship: a comparison" In Maurice Freedman, editor, Family and Kinship in Chinese Society. Stanford, Calif.: Stanford University Press. Pp. 227–48.
Perry, Helen Swick and Mary Ladd Gawel (editors)
   1953 The Interpersonal Theory of Psychiatry. New York: Norton.
Plath, David W.
   1964 "Where the Family of God is the family: the role of the dead in Japanese households" American Anthropologist 66, 2: 300–17.
   1975 "Introduction. From the zabuton: a view of personal episodes" In David W. Plath, editor, Adult Episodes in Japan. Journal of Asian and African Studies (Special Number) 10, 1–2: 1–9.
   1980 Long Engagements: Maturity in Modern Japan. Stanford, Calif.: Stanford University Press.
Prime Minister's Statistical Office
   1979 Public Opinion Survey Annual (Seron chōsa nenkan). Tokyo: Sōrifu.
Reischauer, Edwin O.
   1977 The Japanese. Cambridge, Mass.: Harvard University Press.

Roden, Donald T.
1980 Schooldays in Imperial Japan: A Study in the Culture of the Student Elite. Berkeley and Los Angeles: University of California Press.

Rohlen, Thomas P.
1974 For Harmony and Strength: Japanese White-Collar Organization in Anthropological Perspective. Berkeley and Los Angeles: University of California Press.

Rustin, Bayard
1976 "No growth has to mean less is less" New York Times Magazine, May 2.

Ruyle, Eugene E.
1979 "Conflicting Japanese interpretations of the outcaste problem (*buraku mondai*)" American Ethnologist 6, 1: 55–72.

Said, Edward W.
1978 Orientalism. New York: Pantheon.

Shillony, Ben-Ami
1981 Politics and Culture in Wartime Japan. Oxford: Oxford University Press.

Siemes, Johannes
1968 Hermann Roesler and the Making of the Meiji State. Tokyo: Sophia University.

Silberman, Bernard S.
1974 "Conclusion: Taisho Japan and the crisis of secularism" In Bernard S. Silberman and Harry D. Harootunian, editors, Japan in Crisis: Essays on Taishō Democracy. Princeton, N.J.: Princeton University Press. Pp. 437–53.

Singer, Kurt
1973 Mirror, Sword and Jewel: A Study of Japanese Characteristics. New York: Braziller.

Smith, Robert J.
1962a "Japanese kinship terminology: the history of a nomenclature" Ethnology 1, 3: 349–58.
1962b "Stability in Japanese kinship terminology: the historical evidence" in Robert J. Smith and Richard K. Beardsley, editors, Japanese Culture: Its Development and Characteristics. Chicago: Aldine. Pp. 25–33.
1972 "Small families, small households, and residential instability:

town and city in 'pre-modern' Japan" In Peter Laslett, editor, Household and Family in Past Time: Comparative Studies in the Size and Structure of the Domestic Group over Time. Cambridge University Press. Pp. 429–71.

1974 Ancestor Worship in Contemporary Japan. Stanford, Calif.: Stanford University Press.

1977 "Diversity and variability in Japanese society" Papers in Anthropology, Department of Anthropology, University of Oklahoma 18, 2: 1–9.

1978 Kurusu: The Price of Progress in a Japanese Village, 1951–1975. Stanford, Calif.: Stanford University Press.

Smith, Robert J. and Ella Lury Wiswell
1982 The Women of Suye Mura. Chicago: University of Chicago Press.

Smith, Thomas C.
1961 "Japan's aristocratic revolution" Yale Review 50: 370–83.

Strauss, Anselm (editor)
1956 The Social Psychology of George Herbert Mead. Chicago: University of Chicago Press.

Sugimoto, Yoshio
1980 Popular Disturbance in Postwar Japan. Hong Kong: Asian Research Service.

Suzuki, Takao (translated by Akira Miura)
1978 Japanese and the Japanese: Words in Culture (*Kotoba to bunka*). Tokyo: Kodansha International.

Tada, Michitarō
1978 "The glory and misery of 'my home' " In J. Victor Koschmann, editor, Authority and the Individual in Japan: Citizen Protest in Historical Perspective. Tokyo: University of Tokyo Press. Pp. 207–17.

Taira, Koji
1979 "Review of Robert J. Smith Kurusu: The Price of Progress in a Japanese Village, 1951–1975" Journal of Economic History 39, 2: 569–70.

Takezawa, Shin-ichi and Arthur M. Whitehill
1981 Work Ways: Japan and America. Tokyo: The Japan Institute of Labor.

Tsukahira, Toshio G.
1966 Feudal Control in Tokugawa Japan: The Sankin Kōtai

System. Cambridge, Mass.: Harvard University Press.

Tsunoda, Ryusaku, William Theodore de Bary, and Donald Keene (compilers)
1958 Sources of the Japanese Tradition. New York: Columbia University Press.

Ueda, Makoto
1965 Zeami, Bashō, Yeats, Pound: A Study in Japanese and English Poetics. The Hague: Mouton.

Varley, H. Paul (translator)
1980 A Chronicle of Gods and Sovereigns: Jinnō Shōtōki of Kitabatake Chikafusa. New York: Columbia University Press.

Ware, James R. (translator)
1955 The Sayings of Confucius. New York: New American Library.

Webb, Herschel
1965 "The development of an orthodox attitude toward the imperial institution in the nineteenth century" In Marius B. Jansen, editor, Changing Japanese Attitudes toward Modernization. Princeton, N.J.: Princeton University Press. Pp. 167–91.
1968 The Japanese Imperial Institution in the Tokugawa Period. New York: Columbia University Press.

Weller, Robert P.
1981 Unity and Diversity in Chinese Religious Ideology. Unpublished PhD dissertation, Johns Hopkins University.

Whiting, Robert
1979 "You've gotta have 'wa' " Sports Illustrated, September 24: 60–71.

Wolff, Jonathan H.
1980 Linguistic Socialization, Self, and Personal Referents in Japanese. Unpublished MA dissertation, Cornell University.

Yamamoto, Shichihei
1976 "The living god and his war responsibility" Japan Echo 3, 1: 64–79. (Translated from Shokun, December 1975.)

Yanagita, Kunio
1969 Nihon no matsuri (Japanese Festivals). In Yanagita Kunio shū (The Collected Works of Yanagita Kunio). Tokyo: Chikuma shobō. Volume 10: 155–314.

Yearley, Lee H.
  1980 "Hsun Tzu on the mind: his attempted synthesis of
        Confucianism and Taoism" Journal of Asian Studies 39, 3:
        465–80.
Yukawa, Hideki
  1967 "Modern trends of Western civilization and cultural pecu-
        liarities in Japan" In Charles A. Moore, editor, The
        Japanese Mind: Essentials of Japanese Philosophy and
        Culture. Honolulu: East-West Center Press and University
        of Hawaii Press. Pp. 52–60.
  1973 Creativity and Intuition: A Physicist Looks at East and
        West (translated by John Bester). Tokyo: Kodansha
        International.

Author index

Subject index